Master Your Emotions: The Neuroscience of Emotional Freedom

Arthur Leclairé

Published by Arthur Leclairé, 2025.

MASTER YOUR EMOTIONS: THE NEUROSCIENCE OF EMOTIONAL FREEDOM

First edition. July 11, 2025.

ISBN: 979-8231856527

Written by Arthur Leclairé.

Table of Contents

Introduction

You think you're in control of your emotions. You believe you can handle whatever life throws your way, that you've mastered the art of staying calm and rational when things get tough. But the truth is, your emotions control you far more than you realize.

Sure, you might think you're immune—perhaps even skilled at masking or hiding your feelings. But every time you feel anger flare up, or fear creep in, or anxiety take over, it's those emotions that are quietly steering your actions. Without you even noticing, they shape your decisions, your relationships, and the very course of your life.

Ask yourself—when was the last time you truly felt in command of your emotions? Not simply suppressing them, not letting them sit in the back of your mind while you try to keep your composure, but actually mastering them? Using your emotions as tools, not chains? Most people don't even realize that this level of control is possible, let alone available to them. They'll tell you it's all about "managing" your emotions, but managing isn't the same as mastering. Managing is passive; it's about surviving, not thriving.

Here's the hard truth: if you're like most people, you've never been in full control of your emotions. Maybe you've been able to hide them, distract yourself from them, or simply push through when they get too intense. But real emotional mastery? That's something few ever achieve. And that's exactly what this book is going to change for you.

Emotions are not some unstoppable force of nature, beyond your reach. They are biological processes, driven by specific neural pathways. They can be understood, controlled, and even harnessed—if you know how. You don't need to be a slave to your emotional responses. You don't need to let fear control your decisions, or anger lead you into regret. The truth is, you have the power to rewrite the way your brain handles emotions. And once you do, you'll find yourself not just surviving, but thriving.

The foundation of emotional freedom lies in understanding how your brain works. How the neural circuits responsible for fear, anger, sadness, and happiness all interact. How the chemicals and hormones that surge through your body in response to certain situations can be reprogrammed to stop controlling you. This isn't some distant dream or abstract theory. This is science. This is the art of emotional mastery, and it's grounded in what we know about the brain and how it operates.

Throughout this book, you'll learn how to break the emotional patterns that hold you back. How to spot your triggers before they send you into a spiral. How to detach yourself from the reactions that make you feel weak or out of control. I won't tell you that it's going to be easy, but I will show you that it is possible. It's not about simply "getting better" at handling emotions—it's about transforming how you respond to them, and ultimately, how you let them shape your life.

Most people don't know that emotional freedom is a skill. A skill that can be honed. A skill that requires understanding, practice, and the right tools. But once you master it, you'll see a profound shift. You'll make decisions more clearly. You'll act with more confidence. You'll stop being swayed by every passing emotion, and instead use them to your advantage.

What separates those who succeed from those who fail, in business, in relationships, in life itself, isn't just intelligence or talent. It's emotional control. It's the ability to remain calm under pressure, to not be swept away by the tides of fear or anger, to think and act strategically no matter what you're feeling. This is what makes the difference between living a life dictated by emotions, or living a life guided by reason.

But here's the thing—this isn't some abstract concept. It's not some distant goal you'll reach "someday." It's something you can start learning today, right now. Emotional freedom isn't about suppressing your feelings, ignoring them, or pretending they don't exist. It's about understanding them deeply enough to take charge of them. When you understand why you feel the way you do, when you know how to break free from automatic emotional reactions, you can start making better decisions. You'll begin to see that emotional control isn't just possible—it's inevitable.

And once you have control over your emotions, once you master them, you will unlock a level of clarity and confidence that most people never achieve. You'll no longer be held back by self-doubt or emotional turmoil. Instead, you'll use your emotions as fuel, turning them into a powerful force that propels you forward, not something that holds you back.

This book isn't just about understanding emotions—it's about changing the way you live. It's about becoming the kind of person who no longer reacts, but responds. The kind of person who understands the power of their emotions and uses that power to shape their life, rather than letting their emotions shape them.

Are you ready to take control? Then let's begin.

Chapter 1: The Hidden Power of Your Emotions

The Brain's Hidden Architecture: Why Your Emotions Control You

Emotions, more than any other aspect of your mind, are what dictate your behavior. You may think you're in control—rational, thinking things through—but when emotions kick in, logic often takes a back seat. You've probably heard the phrase, "I wasn't thinking clearly." That's not an accident. It's the brain working exactly the way it's wired to work.

Your brain is a complex system, built over millions of years, designed to help you survive and thrive in an unpredictable world. But the way it handles emotions isn't always so logical. In fact, much of what you feel and do is driven by systems that you don't consciously control. The part of your brain that handles emotions—the limbic system—often operates on autopilot, out of your awareness, making decisions for you before you even realize it.

The Limbic System: The Emotional Control Center

To understand why your emotions control you, you need to understand the brain structures responsible for them. The limbic system is the main center for emotional processing in the brain. It includes structures like the amygdala, hippocampus, and hypothalamus—key players in how you respond to stimuli, both consciously and unconsciously.

The **amygdala** is especially important. It's often referred to as the brain's "emotion center," and for good reason. Its primary job is to evaluate threats and trigger emotional responses, particularly fear. When something happens that could be dangerous, the amygdala reacts. It tells your body to prepare for a fight or flight response, releasing adrenaline and cortisol—hormones that prepare you to act quickly.

But the amygdala doesn't just respond to external threats. It also reacts to internal stimuli, like memories or even thoughts. This means that your emotions don't always match the reality of a situation. You might feel anxious in a social setting because your amygdala associates social situations with past moments of embarrassment or rejection—even if nothing threatening is actually happening.

This happens because the amygdala is quick to act but slow to update its response. If you've experienced something emotionally charged in the past, the amygdala will remember it, and the next time a similar situation arises, it will react in the same way—even if the context has changed. That's why someone might feel terrified of speaking in public or get irrationally angry when someone disagrees with them. The amygdala is locked into an old pattern, and it reacts as though the past is still happening in the present.

Next, there's the **hippocampus**. Its role is to store and retrieve memories, and it works closely with the amygdala. When an emotional event happens, the hippocampus helps the brain store that memory and tag it with an emotional response. The amygdala, in turn, will use that stored information to assess future situations. This creates a cycle: your brain reacts to a situation based on what it remembers, and that emotional reaction reinforces the memory, which strengthens the emotional response next time.

This is why the emotional response to something as simple as a loud noise, a certain smell, or a familiar place can trigger intense feelings—even though there's no real danger in the present moment. The brain has created a connection between the stimulus and the emotional response, and it repeats the pattern automatically.

Unconscious Triggers: The Brain's Hidden Manipulators

What you may not realize is that these reactions aren't always conscious. In fact, much of what you feel is driven by unconscious triggers. Your brain is constantly scanning the environment, picking up cues—whether visual, auditory, or even smells—that remind it of past experiences. When it detects a trigger, it activates the emotional response tied to that memory.

Let's say you walk into a room and the scent of perfume reminds you of a person you once had an argument with. Without even realizing it, your brain processes that scent, retrieves the emotional memory, and triggers the feelings of tension or frustration you experienced during that argument. Your body responds to the emotion before your conscious mind even catches up.

These unconscious triggers can be so powerful that they drive your behavior without your awareness. You might feel uneasy around certain people or places, not because of anything they've done recently, but because your brain is remembering something from the past. It's automatic. You don't have to think about it.

This is why emotional reactions are so difficult to control. They're rooted in systems that bypass your conscious awareness. It's not as simple as deciding to stop feeling anxious, angry, or sad. When those feelings arise, they're being triggered by a complex web of past experiences, memories, and neural pathways that you've built up over time. The unconscious mind is making decisions for you, and you're just along for the ride.

Why Awareness Is Your First Weapon

So, what does this mean for you? If emotions are being triggered unconsciously, and they're influencing your decisions and behaviors before you even realize it, how can you change anything? The answer is simple: awareness.

Awareness is the key to disrupting the cycle. It's the first step in taking control of your emotional life. The reason most people stay trapped in reactive emotional patterns is because they don't even realize these patterns exist. They respond to emotional triggers without ever questioning them. They just feel something and act on it, often with little understanding of why.

The first step in emotional mastery is recognizing the patterns in your own mind. That means taking a step back and looking at your emotional responses—not just when they're obvious, but when they're subtle. When you feel frustrated for no clear reason, or when you feel uneasy in a situation that others seem to handle just fine, that's your chance to ask yourself, "Why am I feeling this way?"

This awareness allows you to begin to trace the pattern. What happened just before the emotion arose? Was it something external, like a comment someone made, or something internal, like a thought or memory? Once you start noticing these patterns, you can begin to interrupt them.

This is where emotional mastery begins. Once you recognize an emotional trigger, you can start to evaluate it. Is the reaction appropriate for the situation? Is the emotion grounded in reality, or is it a result of an old memory or pattern? The more you practice this awareness, the more you'll notice your emotional responses before they control you.

Take a moment to think about a situation where you've lost control of your emotions in the past. It might be a time when you became angry, anxious, or fearful—maybe even when you said or did something you later regretted. Now, think back to what happened just before that. What set you off? Could it have been a small comment, a look, or a feeling you didn't even understand? When you step back and examine it, you'll begin to notice that most emotional responses are based on patterns, not facts.

This awareness isn't a one-time thing. It's something you have to practice daily. But once you begin to notice the unconscious triggers and the emotional responses they set off, you can start to change them. You can learn to pause before reacting, to choose a different response, to ask yourself whether the emotion you're feeling is truly justified by the situation at hand.

The Cycle of Emotion: Breaking Free

Once you become aware of the unconscious triggers, the next step is to break the cycle. If you can identify the pattern—whether it's anger, fear, sadness, or frustration—you can take action to interrupt it. The emotional response doesn't have to be automatic. Instead of reacting immediately, you can pause, assess the situation, and choose a more measured response.

This doesn't mean you'll never feel anger again, or that you'll always remain calm in stressful situations. What it means is that you'll have more control over how you respond. You'll be able to choose whether to react with intensity, or to step back and handle the situation with a clearer mind. This is what it means to master your emotions: the ability to respond, rather than react.

Over time, as you practice awareness and disrupt the emotional cycle, your brain will start to form new, healthier pathways. You'll create new neural connections that prioritize logical thinking and emotional regulation over automatic emotional responses. Eventually, your brain will begin to default to more balanced reactions. Emotional triggers won't have the same power over you because you'll have trained your mind to respond differently.

The key is to start with awareness. Start by noticing when emotions arise, and then ask yourself why. Question your emotional reactions. Over time, this will lead to greater emotional freedom and control. And once you're able to break the cycle of unconscious emotional responses, you'll find that your life begins to shift. You'll make better decisions, act with greater clarity, and become the kind of person who can remain calm, focused, and in control, no matter what happens.

This is the power of awareness. This is the first step in mastering your emotions. And once you've taken that step, you'll begin to see the change.

The Emotional Hijack: How Your Brain Betrays You

When emotions take over, your brain betrays you. It's not just a figure of speech—it's a literal breakdown of the way your brain processes information. In moments of intense emotion, your brain switches into a mode that prioritizes survival over logic, instinct over reason. This is known as **emotional hijacking**, and it happens so quickly that you often don't even realize it's happening until it's too late.

The emotional hijack is not an accident, nor is it a flaw in your brain's design. It's a feature that was essential for survival in ancient times, but in modern life, it often works against us. The problem arises when emotional reactions are triggered by things that have little or nothing to do with actual danger, yet your brain still processes them as though they do. Understanding this process and learning how to recognize when it's happening gives you the power to stop it before it spirals out of control.

The Science Behind Emotional Hijacking: What's Really Happening in Your Brain

The emotional hijack begins with the **amygdala**, a small almond-shaped structure in the brain that plays a key role in processing emotions like fear, anger, and anxiety. The amygdala is wired to react quickly to potential threats, often before you're consciously aware of them. When it senses a danger—whether real or perceived—it sends a signal to the body to prepare for action: fight, flight, or freeze. This is the body's natural stress response, designed to help you deal with immediate danger.

However, here's the problem: in modern life, many of the threats that trigger this reaction aren't life-threatening at all. Your boss raises their voice, someone cuts you off in traffic, or an embarrassing memory resurfaces at the worst possible time. In these cases, the threat is psychological, not physical, but your brain processes it as though it's a matter of life and death. When the amygdala perceives a threat, it bypasses the rational, logical part of the brain—the **prefrontal cortex**—which is responsible for decision-making, problem-solving, and impulse control. The prefrontal cortex is the "thinking brain," while the amygdala is the "reacting brain." When an emotional hijack occurs, the prefrontal cortex essentially shuts down, and the amygdala takes over, flooding your body with chemicals like **adrenaline** and **cortisol**, which are designed to help you respond quickly to danger.

This leads to an immediate physiological response: your heart rate increases, your muscles tense, and your senses sharpen. The problem is, when your brain is hijacked, you're no longer thinking clearly. You're operating purely on instinct, reacting without fully understanding the situation or its consequences. This is why you've probably done things in the heat of the moment that you later regretted. You weren't in control. Your emotions were.

How Emotional Hijacking Impacts Cognition and Behavior

The consequences of emotional hijacking go beyond just feeling upset. When the amygdala takes control, it affects your cognition—how you think and process information. The prefrontal cortex, responsible for higher-level thinking and decision-making, is temporarily overridden, leaving you unable to think critically or rationally. This is why people often make impulsive decisions when angry or frightened. You're not processing information in a logical way; you're reacting emotionally, and it can lead to poor choices.

Let's consider an example. Imagine you're in a meeting, and someone criticizes your work in front of your colleagues. You feel the heat rise in your chest, and suddenly, you're flooded with a mix of anger and embarrassment. Your amygdala immediately kicks in, preparing you to fight back. Your heart rate increases, your breathing becomes shallow, and the words you've been thinking about saying are already forming in your head. In that moment, your prefrontal cortex is out of the picture, and you're operating purely on emotional impulse. You might lash out at your colleague, defend yourself aggressively, or say something you later regret.

What happens next is critical: your brain will replay the moment over and over. The more you replay it, the more you reinforce that emotional reaction. The amygdala strengthens its grip on your behavior, creating a feedback loop that makes it more likely you'll react the same way the next time you feel similar emotions. This cycle of emotional hijacking reinforces poor decision-making and can damage relationships, erode trust, and lead to long-term emotional instability.

Recognizing the First Signs of Emotional Escalation

The first step in preventing an emotional hijack is recognizing the signs before they get out of hand. Most people are unaware of the physiological cues that precede an emotional hijack, but they're there. Your body is constantly sending signals, and the more attuned you are to them, the better you can respond.

Some early warning signs of emotional escalation include:

- **Increased Heart Rate:** One of the first physiological responses to an emotional trigger is an increased heart rate. You may notice your pulse quicken, especially in situations that make you anxious, angry, or excited.
- **Shallow Breathing:** When your body prepares for fight or flight, your breathing often becomes shallow and rapid. You might find yourself gasping for air or taking shorter breaths than usual.
- **Muscle Tension:** Your muscles may tighten in preparation for action. You might clench your fists, jaw, or shoulders, or feel the urge to "tense up" when you feel threatened.
- **Racing Thoughts:** Your mind starts to race, and you feel an overwhelming urge to respond immediately, often without thinking things through. You may become fixated on the perceived threat, which makes it difficult to see the bigger picture.
- **Hot or Cold Sensations:** Your body temperature can fluctuate as the nervous system kicks into gear. You might feel heat in your chest or face if you're angry, or a cold rush if you're fearful or anxious.
- **Tunnel Vision:** When under emotional stress, your attention narrows, and you focus solely on the perceived threat. This can make it difficult to think about anything else or see the full context of the situation.

These signs are often the first indications that an emotional hijack is happening. The key is to notice them early enough to intervene before the emotional escalation gets out of hand. When you begin to feel your heart rate rise or your thoughts race, that's your cue to pause and regain control.

Techniques to Reprogram Your Reactions with Mindfulness

Once you recognize the early signs of an emotional hijack, the next step is to **interrupt** the cycle before it spirals. The most effective way to do this is through **mindfulness**—a practice of bringing your awareness to the present moment and observing your thoughts, feelings, and bodily sensations without judgment. Mindfulness helps you become an observer of your emotions rather than a slave to them.

Here's how you can use mindfulness to regain control:

1. The Power of the Pause

The first step in breaking the cycle of emotional hijacking is learning to pause. When you feel yourself starting to react emotionally, take a moment to stop, breathe, and assess the situation. This pause allows your prefrontal cortex to catch up with your amygdala's impulsive reaction. It creates a gap between stimulus and response—a brief moment where you can choose how to act rather than react.

Even a few seconds of conscious breathing can make a significant difference. As you inhale and exhale slowly, you're signaling to your brain that you're not in immediate danger, that there's no need for an emergency response. The act of breathing deeply calms the body and engages the parasympathetic nervous system, which helps to counteract the fight-or-flight response.

2. Grounding Yourself in the Present

When emotions start to escalate, you might feel disconnected from your surroundings, lost in your thoughts. This is especially common in situations of intense fear or anger, where your mind gets consumed with "what ifs" or worst-case scenarios. Grounding yourself in the present moment helps to disrupt this mental spiral.

One simple grounding technique is to focus on your physical senses. Try to notice five things you can see, four things you can hear, three things you can touch, two things you can smell, and one thing you can taste. This brings your attention to the here and now, preventing your mind from running away with the emotion. It reminds you that you're not in physical danger, and that emotional reactions are just temporary.

3. Reframing the Situation

Once you've taken a moment to pause and ground yourself, the next step is **cognitive reframing**. This involves looking at the situation from a different perspective. Ask yourself: *What else could be true in this situation? What might I be overlooking?*

For example, if you're feeling angry because someone criticized you at work, instead of reacting with defensiveness, try to view it as an opportunity for growth. Could their criticism have some truth to it? Could this be a chance to improve your work or communication skills? Reframing the situation allows you to detach from the immediate emotional response and approach the challenge more rationally.

4. Mindful Acceptance

Lastly, mindful acceptance involves acknowledging your emotions without judgment. Instead of trying to push your feelings away or suppress them, recognize that they are valid. You're feeling angry or anxious, and that's okay. Emotions are part of the human experience. The key is not to let them control you.

Mindful acceptance means accepting your feelings without allowing them to dictate your behavior. You can acknowledge that you're upset, but you don't have to act on it impulsively. This act of self-compassion and understanding creates space for a more measured response.

Reclaiming Your Emotional Autonomy

Emotional hijacking is a natural process, but it doesn't have to control your life. By becoming aware of the signs of emotional escalation and using techniques like mindfulness, you can take back control. You don't need to be at the mercy of your emotions. Instead, you can train your brain to respond in a way that's more rational, measured, and effective. Emotional mastery doesn't mean suppressing your feelings—it means understanding them and choosing how to respond.

By learning to pause, ground yourself, reframe situations, and accept your emotions with mindfulness, you can break the cycle of emotional hijacking and reclaim your autonomy. This is the first step toward emotional freedom: recognizing when your brain betrays you, and learning to stop it before it dictates your behavior.

Your Emotional Ecosystem: Balancing Logic and Feeling

The human mind is not a single entity but a collection of systems, each with its own purpose and its own way of processing information. Emotions are part of that complex system, and they play a critical role in decision-making, behavior, and relationships. But they cannot be allowed to take full control. Likewise, pure logic without the balancing influence of emotions often leads to cold, disconnected decision-making. The key to emotional mastery lies in finding a balance between **logic** and **emotion**—between the thinking mind (the **prefrontal cortex**) and the emotional brain (the **amygdala**).

To understand how to balance the two, you need to look at their functions and how they interact. The amygdala is fast. It reacts quickly to stimuli, almost reflexively. It's what makes you jump when you hear a loud noise or freeze when you sense danger. It's designed for quick, survival-oriented decisions, which is why it's so hard to control in emotionally charged moments. The prefrontal cortex, on the other hand, is slow. It's the part of the brain responsible for higher-order functions like reasoning, planning, and self-control. When the prefrontal cortex is in charge, you're able to think through decisions logically, evaluate situations more thoroughly, and make deliberate choices.

The problem arises when these two systems are out of balance. When the amygdala takes over, emotions dominate, and you're no longer thinking clearly. When the prefrontal cortex is dominant to the exclusion of emotions, decisions can become overly rational, devoid of empathy or emotional intelligence. Achieving emotional mastery requires understanding how both parts of the brain function, and more importantly, how to bring them into harmony.

The Battle Between the Amygdala and the Prefrontal Cortex

When faced with a stressful or emotionally charged situation, your brain doesn't ask you for permission to react. The amygdala takes over almost immediately, prioritizing immediate action over thoughtful consideration. This emotional response often happens before you've even consciously registered what's going on. If someone insults you in a meeting, for instance, the amygdala quickly detects the threat to your sense of self and signals your body to react—anger surges, your heart rate rises, and your body prepares for conflict.

However, the prefrontal cortex, which controls your ability to think, reason, and make decisions, can override the amygdala's impulses. This is the area of your brain responsible for more deliberate responses. If you're able to engage your prefrontal cortex in the moment, you can pause before reacting, consider the consequences of your actions, and choose a more thoughtful response.

Unfortunately, this doesn't always happen, especially when the emotional trigger is strong. When emotions are high, the prefrontal cortex is less able to exercise control over the amygdala. In fact, the brain's wiring often puts emotions first and logic second. This is why you sometimes say things you don't mean, act impulsively, or do things you later regret.

But it's important to remember that emotions, by themselves, are not the enemy. The amygdala's quick reactions are adaptive in situations where immediate action is required—like when you're in physical danger. The problem arises when those reactions occur in situations where logic should have more say, or when you feel compelled to act on emotions that are based on past experiences, rather than the present situation.

To gain control, you need to train yourself to recognize when the amygdala is taking over and deliberately engage your prefrontal cortex to intervene.

Why Emotional Suppression Doesn't Work

The usual advice most people get when dealing with emotions is to suppress them. "Just calm down," they're told, or "Don't get so emotional." The problem with this approach is that it doesn't actually address the root of the issue. Emotional suppression may seem like a quick fix, but it rarely works in the long term. In fact, suppressing emotions only pushes them deeper into the unconscious, where they can continue to affect your behavior in subtle ways.

When you suppress an emotion, you're not addressing its cause, you're only bottling it up. This can create internal conflict. The emotion doesn't go away—it's just buried, waiting for an opportunity to resurface, often in a more intense or unpredictable form. Think of it like a pressure cooker. The more you suppress, the more pressure builds up, until eventually, the lid blows off, and the emotion comes out in an uncontrolled way.

Let's consider an example. Imagine you're frustrated by a colleague's behavior at work. Instead of expressing your frustration or addressing the issue, you suppress it. You push it down, thinking that ignoring it will make it go away. However, that frustration doesn't disappear. Over time, it builds. Your next interaction with the colleague might seem trivial, but because you never dealt with the earlier emotion, the frustration bursts out in an exaggerated, disproportionate response.

This is the danger of emotional suppression: it doesn't allow for the release or resolution of emotions. And when those emotions finally do surface, they often do so in ways that are more damaging than if you'd simply addressed them in the moment.

There's also the issue that suppressed emotions can manifest as physical symptoms—headaches, fatigue, anxiety, or even depression. Research has shown that chronic emotional suppression can take a toll on both your mental and physical health, leading to increased stress and a weakened immune system. It also damages your ability to relate to others, as you become less attuned to your own emotional responses, which affects your empathy and communication skills.

Introducing Emotional Intelligence: The Key to Balancing Logic and Feeling

Instead of suppressing emotions, the solution lies in **emotional intelligence (EI)**—the ability to understand, regulate, and harness emotions in a healthy, productive way. Emotional intelligence involves recognizing your emotions, understanding what they mean, and then choosing how to respond. It doesn't mean suppressing your emotions or letting them dictate your behavior without thought; it's about finding a middle ground where both logic and emotion work together.

The concept of emotional intelligence was first popularized by psychologist Daniel Goleman in the 1990s, and since then, it has become a cornerstone of personal and professional development. Emotional intelligence is made up of several key components:

1. **Self-Awareness:** The ability to recognize your emotions as they arise.

This is the first step toward emotional mastery. If you can name the emotion you're feeling, you can start to understand its cause. This means paying attention to your internal state and becoming aware of emotional triggers before they escalate.

2. **Self-Regulation:** The ability to manage and control your emotional reactions. Self-regulation involves knowing how to pause, take a step back, and think before responding. It's about not letting your emotions control you but choosing how you want to react. This is where the prefrontal cortex comes in. By engaging your thinking brain, you can shift the emotional reaction into a more reasoned response.
3. **Motivation:** Emotional intelligence also involves being able to use your emotions to fuel positive actions. Instead of letting negative emotions derail you, you can channel emotions like frustration or disappointment into motivation to perform better or improve your situation.
4. **Empathy:** Empathy is the ability to understand the emotions of others. This is where the balance between logic and feeling becomes essential. By being able to understand how others are feeling, you can respond in a way that is both emotionally intelligent and considerate, enhancing your relationships and communication skills.
5. **Social Skills:** Social skills involve using your emotional intelligence to manage relationships effectively. This includes things like conflict resolution, collaboration, and leadership. Socially skilled individuals are able to navigate the emotional dynamics of a group and use their understanding of emotions to bring people together.

Emotional intelligence is not just a "soft skill" that looks good on paper; it's a practical tool that can drastically improve your ability to make decisions, solve problems, and communicate with others. Research shows that individuals with high emotional intelligence are more successful in their careers, have better mental health, and experience greater satisfaction in relationships.

How to Build and Strengthen Your Emotional Intelligence

Building emotional intelligence isn't something that happens overnight. It requires consistent effort and practice. Here are a few strategies you can use to strengthen your emotional intelligence:

1. **Mindfulness Practice:** Mindfulness is essential for developing self-awareness. It involves paying attention to your thoughts, feelings, and physical sensations without judgment. Regular mindfulness practice allows you to notice when emotions arise and gain insight into their causes. This practice creates space between stimulus and response, giving you the ability to choose how to act rather than react.
2. **Journaling:** Writing about your emotions can help you better understand them. Journaling allows you to process your feelings, reflect on why you felt the way you did, and identify patterns in your emotional responses. Over time, this helps build self-awareness and self-regulation.
3. **Emotional Reframing:** Reframing involves looking at a situation from a different perspective. For instance, if you're feeling angry about something that happened at work, try to view the situation through the eyes of others involved. Could there be a misunderstanding? Are there factors you might be overlooking? Reframing can help you regulate your emotional response and avoid automatic, reactive behaviors.
4. **Develop Empathy:** To improve your empathy, practice listening to others without judgment. Pay attention to both their words and body language, and try to imagine what they might be feeling. By strengthening your ability to empathize, you increase your capacity for emotional intelligence and improve your interactions with others.
5. **Practice Delayed Gratification:** One of the key aspects of emotional regulation is learning how to delay immediate gratification in favor of long-term goals. This could mean holding off on reacting impulsively in a stressful situation or practicing patience in your daily life. The more you practice self-control in small moments, the stronger your emotional intelligence becomes.

Creating a Balanced Emotional Ecosystem

In order to master your emotions, you need to strike a balance between logic and emotion. The prefrontal cortex and the amygdala must work together. Neither one should dominate. Emotional intelligence gives you the tools to regulate your emotions in a way that empowers you to make better decisions, improve your relationships, and achieve your goals. It's not about suppressing emotions or ignoring logic—it's about finding the right balance that works for you.

By strengthening your emotional intelligence, you can prevent your emotions from hijacking your decisions. You can learn to use emotions to your advantage rather than letting them control you. And in doing so, you gain the freedom to respond to life's challenges with greater clarity, composure, and confidence.

Chapter 2: Mastering Your Reactions (The Art of Emotional Control)

The Neuroscience of Self-Regulation: Taming Your Inner Storm

In the face of an emotional storm, there's a simple truth: you have a choice. Whether it's anger flaring up during an argument, anxiety creeping in before a big presentation, or sadness threatening to overwhelm you after a personal setback, the ability to regulate your emotions—**self-regulation**—is what separates reactive, impulsive behavior from calm, measured responses.

Self-regulation doesn't mean suppressing emotions or pretending you don't feel something. It means knowing how to manage your emotional state, how to stay composed even when the pressure is mounting, and how to prevent your emotions from hijacking your rational thinking. But self-regulation doesn't come naturally to everyone. Some people seem to have a knack for staying calm under pressure, while others are prone to emotional outbursts. The good news is that emotional self-regulation is a skill—a skill that can be learned and improved with understanding and practice.

To grasp how you can better regulate your emotions, it's essential to understand how the brain handles them. Emotions are not random bursts of energy; they're physiological reactions triggered by a complex web of neural circuits. By understanding the mechanisms at play, you can learn how to influence them—how to interrupt the cycle of reactivity and take control of your emotional responses.

How the Brain Handles Emotional Regulation

The brain is constantly processing information. Every sensory input, every thought, and every memory creates a cascade of neural activity, much of which is invisible to your conscious mind. Emotions arise when the brain interprets these inputs as significant—either rewarding or threatening. These interpretations happen quickly and automatically, but the key to emotional self-regulation lies in the **prefrontal cortex**, the part of the brain that controls higher-order thinking, decision-making, and impulse control. When the prefrontal cortex is engaged, it can counterbalance the more primitive parts of the brain, like the **amygdala**, which is responsible for generating emotional reactions.

The amygdala's primary function is to detect threats. If it senses something dangerous, it activates a fight-or-flight response, preparing your body for action. This is a very useful mechanism in situations of genuine danger. But when there's no real threat—when the danger is simply a stressful situation, like a difficult conversation or a deadline at work—the amygdala's response is overblown. This is when emotional regulation becomes important. The prefrontal cortex, which sits right behind your forehead, is responsible for overriding that automatic emotional response.

The challenge, of course, is that the amygdala often responds more quickly than the prefrontal cortex. When faced with a stressful situation, the emotional brain kicks in almost immediately, sometimes before the thinking brain even has a chance to process what's happening. This is why people often react impulsively, say things they regret, or feel overwhelmed by their emotions in the heat of the moment.

However, the prefrontal cortex is not powerless. In fact, it has a direct influence on how the amygdala responds. The more you practice emotional self-regulation, the stronger your prefrontal cortex becomes in managing emotional responses. You train your brain to remain composed even when emotions are running high, and over time, your emotional reactivity decreases.

The Role of the Vagus Nerve and Cortisol in Emotional States

The brain isn't the only system involved in emotional regulation. Your **nervous system** plays a huge role in how your body and mind handle emotions. The vagus nerve, a key part of the parasympathetic nervous system, is often referred to as the "brake" of the nervous system. It helps to calm down the body's fight-or-flight response, reducing heart rate and promoting a sense of relaxation. The vagus nerve is also responsible for regulating your breath, and as you breathe slowly and deeply, you activate this nerve, which helps to turn down the intensity of your emotional responses.

In moments of emotional escalation, the vagus nerve can help you regain control by triggering the relaxation response. When you slow down your breathing or practice techniques like deep abdominal breathing, you engage the vagus nerve and signal to your brain that you are no longer in danger. This act of calming the body can have a profound impact on how you perceive and respond to a situation.

On the opposite side of the equation, **cortisol**—the stress hormone—plays a significant role in emotional regulation. When you're stressed, your adrenal glands release cortisol, preparing your body to face a challenge. Cortisol increases your heart rate, heightens alertness, and sharpens focus. However, prolonged exposure to high cortisol levels, like when you're constantly under stress, can have negative effects on the body and mind. Elevated cortisol over time is linked to anxiety, depression, and other emotional difficulties.

The key to emotional regulation is keeping cortisol levels in check. If you're constantly stressed, or if you struggle to recover from stress, your body and mind remain in a heightened state of alert, making it harder to maintain emotional composure. Fortunately, there are several strategies you can use to manage cortisol levels and reduce the impact of stress on your emotional state.

Techniques for Lowering Emotional Reactivity and Maintaining Composure Under Pressure

1. **Deep Breathing**

One of the simplest and most effective techniques for self-regulation is **deep breathing**. It sounds deceptively simple, but it works because it directly activates the vagus nerve, which helps to calm the body and mind. By taking slow, deliberate breaths—especially deep abdominal breaths—you send a signal to your brain that everything is okay, that there's no immediate danger.

The trick is to breathe slowly, filling your lungs with air and then exhaling fully. Try this: inhale for a count of four, hold your breath for a count of four, and then exhale slowly for a count of four. This technique, known as **box breathing**, helps slow down the heart rate, reduce the production of stress hormones, and promote a sense of calm.

This technique is powerful because it can be done anywhere, at any time. When you find yourself in a stressful situation—whether it's a difficult conversation, a high-pressure meeting, or an emotional trigger—taking a few moments to focus on your breath can help bring your emotions back under control.

1. **Mindfulness and Self-Awareness**

Mindfulness is another essential tool for emotional self-regulation. It involves observing your thoughts, feelings, and physical sensations in the present moment, without judgment. Mindfulness is not about suppressing emotions but about acknowledging them without letting them control you. When you practice mindfulness, you become more aware of your emotional state, which gives you the ability to pause and reflect before reacting.

Mindfulness can be practiced through meditation, but you can also practice it in everyday situations. For example, when you feel yourself becoming upset, take a moment to notice what's happening in your body. Are your shoulders tense? Is your heart racing? Are you holding your breath? By tuning into these physical cues, you can recognize the early signs of emotional escalation and take steps to manage them before they spiral out of control.

1. **Cognitive Reframing**

Cognitive reframing is a technique that involves changing the way you perceive a situation. When you feel emotionally triggered, you may automatically interpret the situation in a way that fuels your emotional reaction. For example, if a colleague criticizes your work, you might immediately think, "They don't like me" or "I'm not good enough." These automatic thoughts fuel emotional reactivity.

Cognitive reframing involves challenging these negative thoughts and replacing them with more balanced, realistic perspectives. For example, instead of thinking, "They don't like me," try reframing it as, "They're giving me feedback, and I can use it to improve." By changing your perspective, you change the emotional response, making it easier to stay calm and composed.

1. **Progressive Muscle Relaxation**

Progressive muscle relaxation (PMR) is another technique that can help reduce emotional reactivity. It involves tensing and then relaxing different muscle groups in your body, starting from your feet and working up to your head. By focusing on the tension and release in your muscles, you help to break the cycle of physical stress and induce a state of relaxation.

PMR works because stress often manifests physically, and relaxing your muscles sends a signal to your brain that it's safe to calm down. This is a particularly useful technique when you're feeling physically tense or anxious but can be used to complement deep breathing and mindfulness practices.

1. **Physical Exercise**

Regular physical activity is one of the best ways to manage stress and regulate emotions. Exercise helps to lower cortisol levels and increase the production of **endorphins**, which are natural mood-boosters. Whether it's going for a run, practicing yoga, or lifting weights, exercise helps to release pent-up energy and reduce the physiological effects of stress.

Even short bursts of exercise can have a positive effect. If you're feeling overwhelmed or emotionally triggered, a quick walk or a few minutes of stretching can help bring your emotions back into balance. Exercise helps you release tension in the body, and it can provide a mental break from stressors.

1. **Social Support and Talking It Out**

Sometimes, emotional regulation is about leaning on others. Talking to a friend, family member, or colleague can help you process emotions and gain perspective. Verbalizing your feelings helps you step back from the emotional intensity and see things more clearly. Social support activates the **oxytocin** system in the brain, which promotes feelings of calm and safety.

But it's important to choose your confidants wisely. Talking to someone who is empathetic and nonjudgmental will help you process emotions in a healthy way, while talking to someone who dismisses or invalidates your feelings can make emotional regulation harder.

Mastering Self-Regulation

Self-regulation is not about eliminating emotions but about gaining control over how you respond to them. By understanding how the brain and body work together to produce emotional states, you can employ specific techniques to lower emotional reactivity and maintain composure under pressure. Through deep breathing, mindfulness, cognitive reframing, physical relaxation, and exercise, you can learn to stay calm and focused, even in the most challenging situations.

By building your self-regulation skills, you'll not only improve your emotional well-being but also your ability to make better decisions, navigate difficult situations, and respond to life's challenges with confidence and composure. It's not about avoiding emotions—it's about handling them with wisdom.

The Power of Detachment: Removing Yourself from Emotional Triggers

Emotions, as much as they can enrich our experience of life, have a way of clouding our judgment when left unchecked. You've likely experienced it at some point—an argument with someone you care about that escalates unnecessarily, or feeling paralyzed by anxiety before an important task. These are moments where your emotions take charge, and it can feel as though you're no longer in control of yourself. You might find yourself swept up in anger, frustration, or fear, with no clear way to regain control.

The problem with being swept away by emotions is that it distorts your perception of reality. Emotional triggers—whether they come from a person, a situation, or even your own internal thoughts—pull you into a reactionary state, where instinct and immediate feeling dictate your response. This is where **detachment** becomes essential: the ability to step back from an emotionally charged situation and regain your perspective, instead of being swept away by the current of your feelings. Detachment isn't about suppressing your emotions or distancing yourself from the world around you. It's about gaining control of your reactions by altering the way you engage with emotional triggers. It's about choosing not to be ruled by your feelings.

I'll explain the concept of **cognitive distancing**, which allows you to detach from your emotional triggers, and I'll show you how to use **cognitive reframing** to change the way you interpret emotional events. Lastly, I'll provide practical exercises that you can use to practice detachment and emotional regulation in real-life situations.

Cognitive Distancing: Creating Space Between You and Your Emotions

When an emotional trigger arises, whether it's a harsh comment, an unexpected change, or a stressful situation, your initial reaction is often automatic. The mind tends to respond quickly, without pause, especially in situations that challenge your sense of security or self-worth. But emotional mastery requires slowing that reaction down, creating **space** between the stimulus (the trigger) and your response. **Cognitive distancing** is the technique that helps you do this.

At its core, cognitive distancing is the process of **mentally stepping away** from the emotions you're experiencing. Instead of being consumed by them, you create a psychological distance between yourself and the emotional experience. This doesn't mean denying your feelings, but rather recognizing that your emotions are temporary and not necessarily an accurate reflection of reality. Just because you feel something doesn't mean you have to act on it, or that the feeling defines you.

One of the key ways to practice cognitive distancing is to remind yourself that **you are not your emotions**. Emotions come and go—they are transient states of mind, not permanent fixtures. By mentally acknowledging that your feelings are not your identity, you can begin to detach from them. You can recognize that you're experiencing an emotion—be it anger, frustration, fear, or sadness—but you don't have to be controlled by it.

The Science Behind Cognitive Distancing

Cognitive distancing works because it helps to engage the **prefrontal cortex**, the part of the brain responsible for rational thinking and impulse control. When emotions run high, the **amygdala**, the brain's emotional center, can hijack the brain, leading to impulsive actions and distorted thinking. But by practicing cognitive distancing, you effectively "turn down" the volume on the amygdala's signal, and allow the prefrontal cortex to take the lead.

When you detach from your emotions, you allow yourself to think more clearly, evaluate the situation more objectively, and ultimately make better decisions. This is the science of **cognitive control**—the ability to control your thoughts and, by extension, your emotions. Cognitive distancing helps you create a mental barrier between the emotional storm and your rational mind.

Research has shown that individuals who are able to distance themselves from their emotions have better outcomes in high-stress situations. They're less likely to act impulsively, more likely to make thoughtful decisions, and better able to navigate difficult social interactions. Cognitive distancing provides the mental clarity necessary for self-regulation, allowing you to make rational decisions even when your emotions are strong.

The Power of Cognitive Reframing

Another powerful technique for detaching from your emotions is **cognitive reframing**. Cognitive reframing involves changing the way you interpret a situation in order to alter your emotional response. Instead of automatically reacting to a situation based on your initial interpretation, reframing allows you to step back and view the situation from a different angle.

Let's say you receive a critical email from your boss. At first, your mind might jump to the conclusion that your boss is upset with you, that you've failed in some way, or that your job is at risk. These interpretations will likely trigger feelings of anxiety, self-doubt, or frustration. However, if you practice cognitive reframing, you can change your interpretation of the situation. You might reframe the email by reminding yourself that feedback is an opportunity to improve, not necessarily a personal attack. You might even consider that the email was written in a hurry, and that your boss didn't intend for it to sound as harsh as it does. By changing your interpretation, you can shift your emotional response from fear or anxiety to a more neutral or even positive feeling, such as curiosity or motivation.

Cognitive reframing works by challenging your **automatic thoughts**—those reflexive, knee-jerk reactions you have to situations. These thoughts are often based on assumptions, past experiences, and emotional biases, and they distort the way you perceive reality. Reframing gives you the power to question these assumptions and come to a more balanced, rational conclusion. In doing so, you break the automatic emotional chain reaction and replace it with a more constructive mindset.

How to Practice Cognitive Reframing

The first step in practicing cognitive reframing is to **notice** your emotional reaction. This requires self-awareness. You need to recognize when you're experiencing an emotional response and then pause for a moment to assess the situation. What are you feeling? Why are you feeling it? What thoughts are running through your mind? Once you identify the emotion and the thought associated with it, you can start the reframing process.

Ask yourself questions like:

- What other ways could I interpret this situation?
- What's the most balanced, logical perspective I can take?

- How would I see this situation if I weren't emotionally involved?
- What can I learn from this situation?

By actively challenging your initial emotional reaction, you can disrupt the cycle of reactivity and replace it with a more thoughtful, deliberate response. It takes practice, but over time, you'll become more skilled at reframing situations in real-time, preventing your emotions from taking control.

Practical Exercises for Detachment

Now that you understand cognitive distancing and reframing, let's look at some practical exercises that you can use to practice detachment and emotional regulation in real-life scenarios.

1. **The "Third-Person Perspective" Exercise**

One of the simplest ways to practice cognitive distancing is to view a situation from a **third-person perspective**. When you're emotionally triggered, try imagining that you're observing the situation from an outsider's point of view. This mental shift helps to create psychological distance between you and the emotional experience, allowing you to see the situation more objectively.

For example, if you're feeling angry after a confrontation with a friend, try to imagine that you're a neutral observer watching the interaction from the outside. How would you interpret the conversation if you weren't personally involved? What do you think the other person's perspective might be? This exercise helps you detach from your emotional reaction and gain a clearer, more balanced understanding of the situation.

1. **The "What Would I Advise a Friend?" Exercise**

Another useful exercise for cognitive distancing involves imagining that you're giving advice to a friend in a similar situation. If you're feeling overwhelmed by a stressful situation, ask yourself, "What would I tell a friend who is experiencing this?" You're likely to offer more rational, measured advice to a friend than you would to yourself in the same situation. This exercise allows you to step outside of your emotional response and tap into a more logical, objective mindset.

For example, if you're feeling anxious about an upcoming presentation, imagine that a friend is in your position. You might tell them that it's normal to feel nervous but that they should focus on preparation, practice deep breathing, and remind themselves that they are capable. This advice, which is calm and reasonable, is the same kind of perspective you need to apply to yourself.

1. **The "Reframing Journal" Exercise**

A great way to reinforce cognitive reframing is through journaling. Whenever you encounter an emotionally charged situation, take a few minutes to write about it. Start by describing the situation and how you felt. Then, ask yourself: "What was my automatic interpretation of this situation?" "What assumptions did I make?" "How could I reframe this situation in a more balanced, constructive way?"

By journaling your thoughts and emotions, you create a space to process and reflect on the situation. You can write about your emotional triggers and the thoughts that accompany them, and then consciously reframe those thoughts. Over time, this exercise helps you to recognize patterns in your emotional responses and develop healthier ways of interpreting events.

1. **The "Pause and Breathe" Exercise**

Before reacting to an emotional trigger, practice taking a moment to **pause** and breathe. It sounds simple, but this exercise is incredibly powerful. When you're triggered by something, instead of jumping to a reaction, take a deep breath, count to three, and allow yourself a brief mental pause. This moment of detachment gives you the space to assess the situation, question your initial emotional response, and decide how to proceed more thoughtfully.

For example, if someone cuts you off in traffic, instead of immediately feeling angry or upset, take a deep breath and pause. Ask yourself: "Is this worth getting upset about? What's the bigger picture here?" Often, a brief moment of reflection can help you detach from the emotional intensity of the situation.

Detachment as a Path to Emotional Freedom

The power of detachment lies in your ability to **choose** how you respond to emotional triggers. Cognitive distancing and reframing are two key tools that can help you break free from the automatic emotional responses that so often dictate your actions. By practicing detachment, you create the space needed to think clearly, make better decisions, and avoid being overwhelmed by your emotions.

Detachment doesn't mean you stop feeling—it means you stop being controlled by your feelings. When you learn to detach, you gain the freedom to engage with life's challenges from a place of emotional strength, rather than reaction.

The "Pause" Technique: Developing a Micro-Second Delay to Control Responses

Emotions often have a way of pulling you into automatic responses. It's like you can feel your body reacting before your mind has time to even process what's happening. This is especially dangerous in moments when a rash decision or impulsive action could have lasting consequences. Imagine you're in a heated discussion and your anger flares. You feel your body tensing, your heart rate rising, and your thoughts spiraling into defensiveness. Without a moment's pause, you might blurt out something you regret—an insult, an overreaction, or something that worsens the situation.

This automatic reaction is common. It's part of how your brain is wired. But what if you could disrupt that cycle? What if you could introduce a simple, almost imperceptible delay between the stimulus (the emotional trigger) and your response? This is where the **Pause Technique** comes into play. It's about giving yourself a micro-second to **stop**, to **breathe**, and to make a more deliberate decision about how to react. It's about creating a tiny gap between your impulse and your action—enough time to regain control before things spiral out of hand.

I will walk you through the **neuroscientific basis** for the pause, how you can build the habit of pausing in emotional decision-making, and the proven research behind creating space between stimulus and reaction. This isn't just theoretical. It's a practical, effective method backed by science, one that you can start implementing in your everyday life.

The Neuroscience of the Pause: How It Works

When you experience an emotional trigger, the **amygdala**, the emotional center of your brain, responds almost instantly. The amygdala detects threats or perceived dangers and sends out an urgent signal for action. This is the famous "fight-or-flight" response that's been hardwired into our brains over millions of years. If someone insults you or a stressful situation arises, the amygdala acts first—often before your rational mind has even had a chance to get involved.

However, the **prefrontal cortex**, the area responsible for rational thinking, impulse control, and decision-making, is slower to engage. It's not as fast as the amygdala, and in a moment of emotional intensity, it's often overwhelmed by the immediate, raw emotional response. This is where the **pause** becomes critical.

In neuroscience, this concept is known as **cognitive control**—the ability of the prefrontal cortex to override or modulate the impulsive reactions of the amygdala. By introducing a deliberate pause, you give your prefrontal cortex the time it needs to engage, process the situation, and decide on a more rational response.

Here's how the process works:

1. **Emotional Trigger (Stimulus)**: Something happens that triggers an emotional response—a harsh comment, a stressful situation, or a personal setback.
2. **Amygdala Response (Reaction)**: The amygdala reacts automatically, generating a strong emotional reaction. This is your body's way of preparing for action, often based on past experiences or learned responses.
3. **The Pause (Delay)**: This is the critical moment. By taking a split second to pause, you disrupt the automatic process. It's like pressing the "brakes" before you crash into a decision or action.
4. **Prefrontal Cortex Activation (Control)**: The pause allows your prefrontal cortex to kick in. With a bit of time to breathe, you can evaluate the situation more rationally, choose a more appropriate response, and break the cycle of impulsivity.

It's this split-second of delay that creates a window of opportunity for you to make a better decision. But it's not just about having the chance to think. The pause literally changes how your brain processes the situation. By intervening with a pause, you shift the dynamics from impulsivity (amygdala-driven) to thoughtful consideration (prefrontal cortex-driven).

Building the Habit of Pause: How to Implement It

Creating the habit of pausing is a skill, one that can be developed with practice. The most challenging part of the pause technique is that it requires **awareness**—you need to recognize when you're being triggered emotionally and when a response is about to happen. That's easier said than done when emotions are high, but the more you practice, the more automatic the pause becomes.

The first step is to **recognize your emotional triggers**. Start by paying attention to moments when you feel your emotions taking over. This might be in response to something someone says, a deadline that's creeping up, or even your own negative self-talk. It doesn't matter if the situation is big or small; the key is to start identifying the emotional moments when you typically react impulsively.

Next, **practice the pause**. Once you're aware of a trigger, your goal is to introduce a small delay before you react. This doesn't mean you have to be physically still or motionless. It's a mental pause. It could be as simple as taking a **deep breath**, counting to three, or silently telling yourself, "Pause." You could also practice mindfulness in these moments, focusing on the present moment rather than the emotional storm brewing in your mind. The key is to break the automatic flow and introduce that micro-second of space.

For example, if you're in an argument with a friend and you feel anger bubbling up, rather than responding immediately with something defensive, you could silently count to three or take a deep breath before speaking. This tiny action buys you time and allows you to process the situation, so you can decide how to respond more effectively.

In some situations, the pause might be more than just a few seconds. You might need to take a break entirely from the situation—a few minutes to cool down or regain your perspective. Sometimes, especially in high-pressure situations, the pause could last longer than expected, and that's perfectly fine. The more you practice it, the more you'll develop an intuitive sense of when and how to take that step back.

Examples from Psychology and Neurofeedback: Creating Space Between Stimulus and Reaction

The effectiveness of the pause technique has been validated by both **psychology** and **neurofeedback research**. In psychology, one of the foundational theories for controlling emotional responses is called **cognitive-behavioral therapy (CBT)**. CBT emphasizes the importance of recognizing and challenging automatic thoughts that trigger emotional reactions. When you learn to pause, you're effectively doing what CBT recommends: intervening in the automatic response cycle before it escalates. Studies have shown that people who use techniques like cognitive reframing and pausing before reacting experience lower levels of stress and more controlled emotional responses.

In **neurofeedback research**, the concept of creating space between stimulus and response is taken a step further. Neurofeedback training teaches individuals to alter their brainwave patterns in real time, helping them develop more control over their emotional and cognitive states. One of the key findings in neurofeedback research is that **brain waves**—specifically **alpha waves** (associated with calm and relaxed states)—can be trained to increase, even in situations that would normally cause stress or agitation. The pause technique mimics this process: by creating space between a trigger and your reaction, you give your brain the opportunity to enter a calmer, more controlled state before acting.

For instance, a 2009 study on neurofeedback and emotional regulation found that individuals who trained their brain waves to be more in sync with the alpha rhythm were better able to manage their emotional responses to stressors. These individuals exhibited more emotional stability and were less likely to react impulsively when faced with difficult situations. The idea is that when you pause, you essentially give your brain the time it needs to reset, much like the neurofeedback training reset the individuals' brainwaves. In both cases, the intervention creates space between emotional activation and the response, allowing for more deliberate and controlled actions.

Practical Applications: Pausing in Real-Life Scenarios

To put the theory into practice, let's look at a few examples of how the pause technique can be applied in everyday situations:

1. **Workplace Stress**: Imagine you're working on a tight deadline, and you receive an email from your boss with a critical comment. Your

first instinct might be to feel defensive or anxious. By pausing before reacting, you allow yourself time to take a breath and choose a more measured response. Perhaps instead of replying immediately with an explanation or a defensive statement, you can first assess the tone of the email, remind yourself that feedback is an opportunity for growth, and craft a thoughtful, professional response.

2. **Relationship Conflicts**: In any relationship, it's easy for emotions to flare up during a disagreement. If your partner says something that triggers an emotional response, like anger or hurt, your automatic reaction might be to lash out or shut down. The pause gives you the moment to stop, assess your emotional state, and decide how you want to handle the situation. You might take a few seconds to breathe, or even excuse yourself for a moment, allowing the intensity of the emotion to subside before you engage in the conversation again.
3. **Public Speaking or Presentations**: You're about to speak in front of an audience, and your nerves are through the roof. Your heart races, your palms sweat, and your mind floods with negative thoughts. Instead of diving into the presentation with a panicked state, take a few moments to pause. You can close your eyes for a moment, take a deep breath, and tell yourself to relax. This small act of pausing gives you a sense of control, reduces the physical symptoms of anxiety, and puts you in a better position to deliver your message clearly.
4. **Anger in Traffic**: If you're stuck in traffic and someone cuts you off, your automatic reaction might be anger. Instead of immediately honking your horn or speeding up to retaliate, the pause allows you to reflect on the situation and decide whether it's worth reacting at all. You may realize that the other driver's behavior isn't something worth getting upset about, and you can proceed without letting the anger take over.

The Power of the Pause

The pause is a deceptively simple but profoundly effective tool for managing emotional responses. By creating space between stimulus and reaction, you give yourself the opportunity to step back, assess the situation, and respond thoughtfully. The pause doesn't just stop you from reacting impulsively; it gives your brain the time it needs to shift from emotional impulsivity to rational control.

Through practice, you can develop the habit of pausing, turning it into a reflexive action that will allow you to handle emotionally charged situations with more composure, clarity, and confidence. The pause might seem small, but its impact on your decision-making, relationships, and emotional well-being is far from insignificant.

Chapter 3: Emotional Freedom through Self-Awareness

Recognizing Your Emotional Patterns: The Key to Breaking Free

You've likely experienced it before: you find yourself reacting to a situation in the exact same way, even though you've promised yourself not to. It could be snapping at a loved one when you're frustrated, shutting down when someone challenges you, or feeling hopeless when something goes wrong. These reactions are automatic, and they seem to happen almost without your control. The truth is, these emotional responses are patterns—habitual ways of thinking, feeling, and acting that your brain has learned over time. The issue, of course, is that these patterns can be **destructive**. They limit your emotional flexibility and can keep you trapped in unhealthy cycles that affect your well-being, relationships, and overall happiness.

The key to breaking free from these emotional traps lies in recognizing **your emotional patterns**. Understanding how these patterns form in your brain—and why they're so difficult to change—gives you the power to rewrite them. Emotional patterns are not just feelings; they are habits of thinking and reacting that have become ingrained in your neural circuitry. And just like any other habit, they can be unlearned.

We'll dive into how the brain forms emotional patterns, why they're so hard to break, and how to map your emotional triggers. I'll also provide practical **self-reflection exercises** to help you identify and **rewire** unhealthy emotional habits. By understanding the underlying processes of emotional patterns, you'll gain the insight and tools necessary to change the way you respond to the world.

How the Brain Forms Emotional Patterns

To understand why emotional patterns are so hard to break, we first need to look at how they form in the first place. Your brain is an incredibly efficient organ. It's always looking for ways to conserve energy and make processes easier.

This is why the brain tends to form **habits**—including emotional habits—over time. Emotional patterns are formed in the brain through a process known as **neuroplasticity**. This refers to the brain's ability to reorganize itself by forming new neural connections in response to experience.

When you experience an emotion, the brain is processing and storing that emotional information. This might seem abstract, but it's not. For example, when you feel fear in response to a stressful situation, your amygdala (the brain's emotional center) processes that fear and sends signals throughout your body. If this happens repeatedly in similar situations, the brain forms a neural pathway. This pathway essentially becomes a "shortcut" for the brain—every time a similar situation arises, the brain quickly activates the same neural pathway, triggering the same emotional response.

In other words, your emotional responses are **reinforced** by repetition. Each time you react in a certain way, your brain strengthens the connections between neurons involved in that response. This is why emotional responses can feel automatic—they are. The more often you experience a particular emotion in response to a certain stimulus, the more ingrained the pattern becomes. Over time, these patterns become part of your emotional **default setting**. You don't have to think about them; you just react.

But the more ingrained these patterns become, the more **rigid** they also become. The brain resists change, especially when the patterns have been reinforced over time. That's why it's so difficult to change your emotional reactions, even when you know they're not serving you. You might want to stop feeling anxious in social situations or stop getting defensive when someone disagrees with you. But your brain has already developed a "habit" of responding in those ways, and it's much easier for the brain to continue using these established pathways than to create new ones.

Why Emotional Patterns Are Hard to Break

Breaking emotional patterns is difficult for two primary reasons: **neural reinforcement** and **the emotional brain's primacy**.

1. **Neural Reinforcement**: As mentioned earlier, every time you experience an emotion, the brain strengthens the neural connections related to that emotion. Over time, the brain forms **pathways** that become deeply entrenched. When you encounter a similar situation,

your brain fires up the same pathway, triggering the same response. For example, if you've experienced repeated instances of rejection or failure in the past, your brain might form a pathway that leads to feelings of inadequacy or anxiety whenever you face a challenge in the future. The more you experience that emotional response, the stronger the neural connection becomes, and the more automatic the reaction feels.

2. **The Emotional Brain's Primacy**: The amygdala, responsible for processing emotions, operates much faster than the prefrontal cortex, the part of the brain involved in rational thinking. This means that when an emotional trigger is present, your brain often responds before you have the chance to think it through. The amygdala is designed to protect you by reacting quickly to perceived threats—whether real or imagined. As a result, emotional reactions can feel overpowering, and the ability to think through them becomes secondary. Your prefrontal cortex might be trying to reason with you, but it can be overpowered by the amygdala's emotional impulses. This creates a cycle of impulsive emotional responses that are difficult to break.

Breaking free from these emotional patterns requires an awareness of how the brain is working against you. But awareness alone isn't enough. The key is to actively interrupt the cycle of neural reinforcement and give the prefrontal cortex the space it needs to take control of the emotional situation.

Mapping Your Emotional Triggers: What's Really Going On in Your Brain?

In order to break free from emotional patterns, you first need to **map your emotional triggers**. These are the events, people, or situations that set off your automatic emotional reactions. Emotional triggers can come from both external sources (such as a conflict with a colleague or a stressful situation) and internal sources (such as negative self-talk or memories from the past). The goal here is to identify these triggers and understand the emotional **feedback loop** they create in your brain.

When a trigger occurs, your brain reacts almost instinctively, activating the neural pathways associated with that emotional response. The key is to **interrupt this loop** before the emotional reaction takes over. Mapping your triggers helps you recognize when these patterns are about to be activated, allowing you to intervene and make a conscious decision about how to respond.

Self-Reflection Exercise: Identifying Your Emotional Triggers

A practical exercise to start mapping your emotional triggers is through **journaling**. At the end of each day, reflect on situations where you felt a strong emotional response. Did you feel anxious, angry, frustrated, or sad? What happened just before you felt that way? Write down the details of the situation, including:

- **Who was involved?**
- **What was said or done?**
- **How did you feel in that moment?**
- **What thoughts crossed your mind during that time?**

The goal is to **pinpoint the exact moment** when the emotional reaction was triggered. Once you identify these moments, ask yourself the following questions:

- What **emotion** did I feel? Is it a pattern? Does it happen in similar situations?
- What **thoughts** came up? Were they rational or distorted?
- Was my reaction automatic, or did I have time to think and decide how to respond?

By regularly journaling about these emotional experiences, you'll begin to notice patterns in your emotional responses. You'll start to see which triggers consistently set off the same emotional reaction, and you can begin to reframe those triggers with **awareness**. Recognizing your emotional triggers is the first step in taking back control.

Self-Reflection Exercise: Rewriting Unhealthy Emotional Habits

Once you've mapped your emotional triggers, the next step is to actively **rewire** your emotional habits. This is where **cognitive reframing** and **mindfulness** come into play.

1. **Cognitive Reframing**: After identifying your emotional triggers, you can start **reframing** the way you think about them. If you're triggered

by criticism from others, instead of viewing it as a personal attack, you can reframe it as an opportunity for growth. Instead of immediately feeling defensive or hurt, reframe the situation as a chance to improve. Ask yourself: "What can I learn from this? How can I use this feedback to become better?"

The goal is to challenge the automatic thoughts that arise with the emotional triggers and replace them with healthier, more balanced thoughts. Reframing helps break the automatic emotional response and shifts the neural pathways toward more constructive ways of thinking and feeling.

1. **Mindfulness**: Another powerful tool for rewiring emotional habits is **mindfulness.** Mindfulness involves being fully present in the moment and observing your thoughts and emotions without judgment. When you experience an emotional trigger, instead of reacting impulsively, practice being present with the emotion. Observe the sensation of anger, fear, or anxiety without labeling it as good or bad. Just allow it to be there. This act of observation creates space between the stimulus and your reaction, and over time, it can help you detach from the habitual emotional responses.

Self-Reflection Exercise: Practice **mindful awareness** in your daily life. When you're triggered by something—whether it's a comment, a situation, or an emotion—take a moment to pause and observe your reaction. What physical sensations do you notice in your body? How does the emotion feel in your chest, stomach, or face? By acknowledging the emotional response without judgment, you can begin to **dissociate** from the automatic reaction and break the cycle.

Breaking Free from Emotional Patterns

The process of breaking free from unhealthy emotional habits requires both awareness and effort. By mapping your emotional triggers and actively intervening in your emotional patterns, you can **rewire** your brain to respond more effectively. This is not about suppressing emotions or pretending they don't exist—it's about gaining **control** over them, so they no longer dictate your actions.

The more you practice recognizing your emotional patterns, the more you'll begin to see that your reactions are not fixed. You can choose how to respond, and with time, you'll develop healthier, more balanced emotional habits. Remember, your brain is capable of change, but it requires consistent effort to break free from the patterns that no longer serve you.

The Neuroscience of Mindfulness: Rewiring Your Brain for Emotional Control

Mindfulness is often presented as some vague, abstract concept—a trendy idea that involves "living in the moment" or "feeling more relaxed." But beneath these surface-level clichés lies a profound **neuroscientific** foundation. Mindfulness isn't just about taking a deep breath or focusing on your surroundings for a few minutes. It's a powerful tool for rewiring your brain, enhancing emotional control, and breaking free from the automatic, impulsive responses that so often lead to regret.

At its core, mindfulness is about **present-moment awareness**—being fully conscious of your thoughts, emotions, and surroundings without judgment. You might think of it as observing your inner world the same way an outsider might observe a scene without getting personally involved in it. The power of mindfulness, however, doesn't just come from the act of noticing; it's the deep, **neuroplastic** changes that occur in your brain when you practice it.

When you begin to train your mind to be more aware of the present moment, you're not only gaining control over your emotional reactions but also strengthening parts of your brain responsible for regulating them. Mindfulness, when practiced regularly, can **rewire neural pathways** to reduce emotional reactivity and improve overall emotional regulation. This makes it an incredibly powerful tool for anyone trying to gain mastery over their emotions.

We'll explore how mindfulness rewires the brain for emotional control, dive into the link between **neuroplasticity** and mindfulness, and provide **actionable mindfulness exercises** that you can start using immediately to take control of your emotional responses.

The Link Between Mindfulness and Neural Plasticity

The brain has a remarkable ability to adapt and change in response to experience. This ability is known as **neuroplasticity**. Simply put, neuroplasticity is the brain's capacity to form new neural connections, reorganize itself, and strengthen or weaken existing pathways. This phenomenon isn't limited to childhood—it continues throughout your life. When you engage in repeated behaviors, thoughts, or practices, you're essentially "shaping" your brain to function in those particular ways.

The practice of mindfulness is one of the most effective methods for inducing neuroplastic change. Regular mindfulness practice strengthens neural circuits involved in attention, emotional regulation, and self-awareness. When you become more aware of your emotional triggers and habitual responses, you begin to interrupt the automatic patterns that were established in your brain over time.

In the context of emotional regulation, mindfulness helps **rewire** the brain by **disrupting** the neural pathways that contribute to impulsive emotional reactions, like anger, anxiety, or defensiveness. Instead of being driven by automatic emotional responses, you start to develop new neural pathways that enable you to respond with greater **calm**, **clarity**, and **self-control**.

Research has shown that practicing mindfulness can lead to significant changes in brain areas responsible for emotional regulation. For example, **neuroimaging studies** reveal that mindfulness practitioners show increased activity in the **prefrontal cortex**—the area of the brain responsible for rational decision-making, impulse control, and higher-order thinking. This is significant because it suggests that mindfulness helps you develop the mental resources to **override** automatic, emotionally driven reactions from the amygdala (the brain's emotional center).

In addition to enhancing prefrontal cortex function, mindfulness practice has been shown to reduce the activity of the **amygdala**. The amygdala is responsible for processing strong emotions like fear, anger, and anxiety. In times of stress, the amygdala can become overactive, leading to heightened emotional reactions. However, mindfulness helps create a more balanced relationship between the amygdala and the prefrontal cortex. By fostering awareness and helping you stay present, mindfulness quiets the amygdala's tendency to hijack your emotional responses.

How Mindfulness Improves Emotional Regulation

At its core, mindfulness helps improve emotional regulation by teaching you how to **observe** your emotions without getting caught up in them. When you're mindful, you recognize emotions as they arise but don't immediately react to them. Instead of being swept away by the force of your emotions, you observe them from a distance. This creates a crucial **gap** between stimulus and response—the space where you can decide how to react.

The reason emotional regulation improves through mindfulness is that it enhances your ability to **pause**, to notice your thoughts and emotions before they spiral into full-blown reactions. This is especially important because **emotional dysregulation** (losing control over your emotions) is often the result of reacting **impulsively** to emotional triggers. By practicing mindfulness, you become aware of your emotions in real-time, enabling you to take that pause and choose a more thoughtful, measured response.

Mindfulness and the Prefrontal Cortex: The "Cooling" System for the Brain

The **prefrontal cortex** plays a critical role in emotional regulation. It's the brain's "cooling system," allowing you to step back, evaluate a situation, and decide how to respond, rather than simply reacting. When you practice mindfulness, you're essentially strengthening your **prefrontal cortex** by giving it more control over the emotional processes that come from the **limbic system** (the area of the brain responsible for emotions).

The prefrontal cortex helps you **override** your immediate emotional impulses. It acts as a "brake" when your emotions threaten to take over, enabling you to respond in ways that are **proportional** to the situation, rather than reacting from a place of fear, anger, or panic. The more you practice mindfulness, the stronger your prefrontal cortex becomes in its ability to exert control over your emotional responses. This means you become less likely to be hijacked by impulsive emotions, and instead, you can stay **calm**, **clear-headed**, and **in control**.

Actionable Mindfulness Exercises for Emotional Mastery

Now that we've established how mindfulness rewires the brain and improves emotional regulation, it's time to put theory into practice. Here are several actionable mindfulness exercises you can use to build emotional control. These exercises are designed to be simple and effective, so you can integrate them into your daily life, no matter how busy you are.

1. The Body Scan: Grounding Yourself in the Present Moment

One of the simplest and most effective mindfulness exercises is the **body scan**. This exercise helps you connect with your body and become more aware of physical sensations, which is an important first step in noticing emotional shifts. When emotions arise, they're often accompanied by physical sensations, such as tension, tightness, or a racing heart. By tuning into these sensations, you can better identify when an emotion is beginning to escalate.

How to do it:

- Sit or lie down in a comfortable position.
- Close your eyes and bring your attention to your body.
- Start by focusing on your toes and gradually work your way up through each part of your body: feet, legs, torso, arms, hands, neck, and head.
- As you focus on each area, simply observe any sensations. You're not trying to change anything; just notice whether you feel tension, warmth, coolness, discomfort, or relaxation.
- If your mind starts to wander, gently bring your focus back to your body.
- Continue this process for 10–15 minutes.

The body scan is effective because it helps you become more aware of the physical signals that precede an emotional reaction. By recognizing these sensations early, you can intervene before the emotion takes over.

2. Labeling Your Emotions: Naming What You Feel

One powerful aspect of mindfulness is being able to label your emotions as they arise. This is not about **suppressing** your emotions or pretending they don't exist. Rather, it's about **acknowledging** what's happening inside you, which reduces the power emotions have over your reactions. When you name an emotion, you gain control over it. It becomes something you observe, rather than something that controls you.

How to do it:

- When you feel an intense emotion, pause for a moment and check in with yourself.
- Ask, "What am I feeling right now?" Try to put a name to the

emotion: anger, sadness, frustration, joy, etc.

- Once you've labeled the emotion, take a few deep breaths. Acknowledge it without judgment. You're not trying to change it; you're simply recognizing it.
- If the emotion is intense, try to pinpoint the **physical sensation** associated with it (e.g., a tight chest or a clenched jaw). This helps you stay connected to the present moment, rather than getting swept up in the emotion.

Labeling emotions helps you gain emotional **awareness** and prevents you from being overwhelmed by them. The act of naming them creates a separation between you and the emotion itself. It allows you to respond, rather than react.

3. The 5-4-3-2-1 Grounding Exercise: Reconnecting to the Present

This exercise is particularly useful when emotions are running high, and you need to quickly regain control. It helps you shift your focus from overwhelming thoughts and emotions to the present moment, using your five senses.

How to do it:

- Take a deep breath and begin by **noticing** five things you can see around you. Look for details you might otherwise overlook, such as the texture of an object or the way light reflects off a surface.
- Next, identify four things you can feel. This might include the sensation of your feet on the floor, the feeling of your clothes against your skin, or the air on your face.
- Then, notice three things you can hear. This might include the hum of a fan, the rustling of papers, or distant voices.
- Afterward, focus on two things you can smell. If you're indoors, this might be the scent of your environment, your coffee, or fresh air.
- Finally, notice one thing you can taste, whether it's the lingering taste of a meal, a drink, or the freshness in your mouth.

By engaging your senses, you create a grounding experience that pulls you back into the present moment. This helps you disrupt emotional escalation and regain a sense of calm and control.

Rewiring Your Brain for Emotional Mastery

Mindfulness is more than just a relaxation technique; it's a tool that can fundamentally change how you experience and regulate your emotions. By practicing mindfulness, you can rewire your brain to respond more thoughtfully and less impulsively to emotional triggers. With regular practice, mindfulness helps you strengthen the **prefrontal cortex**, calm the **amygdala**, and build a more balanced relationship between your thoughts and emotions. The exercises provided in this subchapter are designed to help you become more aware of your emotional patterns and take control of your reactions. Over time, mindfulness will not only improve your emotional regulation but also increase your **self-awareness**, **clarity**, and ability to stay present in every situation. As you continue practicing, you'll find that emotional mastery becomes less of a struggle and more of a natural, intuitive response.

The Mirror Effect: How Self-Perception Shapes Your Emotional Landscape

The way you see yourself has an undeniable influence on how you feel and how you react to the world around you. It's as if there's a mirror in your mind that reflects your beliefs about yourself, and in turn, shapes your emotional state. If you view yourself as incompetent, weak, or unworthy, your emotions will likely follow suit. On the other hand, if you see yourself as capable, confident, and worthy, your emotional responses will tend to be more balanced and resilient. The brain works in a way that reinforces your self-perception, whether it's positive or negative, and the impact this has on your emotional landscape is profound.

This concept, often referred to as the **Mirror Effect**, explains how your internal narrative and beliefs shape the way you experience the world emotionally. If you are constantly telling yourself that you're not good enough, that you're a failure, or that you'll never succeed, your emotional responses will be tinted by those beliefs. You will likely feel anxious, defeated, or demotivated. But if you flip that narrative and start viewing yourself in a more positive light—by recognizing your strengths, achievements, and potential—you'll notice that your emotions begin to shift in a healthier, more resilient direction.

We'll dive into the **neuroscience** behind this phenomenon—how the brain reinforces self-beliefs, why negative self-talk is so damaging, and how you can change the way you perceive yourself to foster emotional resilience. We'll also explore **practical strategies** for overcoming negative self-talk and **strengthening your self-awareness** so that you can build a more positive and balanced emotional landscape.

The Brain's Tendency to Reinforce Self-Beliefs

The brain is wired to maintain consistency. It's a survival mechanism, rooted in the **principle of cognitive consistency**, which states that we tend to seek information and experiences that align with our existing beliefs about ourselves. If you believe you're incompetent, your brain will focus on information or experiences that reinforce this belief. The brain does this not because it's trying to be accurate, but because it values stability and coherence. In this way, your self-perception becomes a **self-fulfilling prophecy**.

The **reticular activating system (RAS)**, a network of neurons in the brainstem, plays a major role in this process. The RAS acts like a filter, prioritizing information that aligns with what you already believe to be true. If you believe you're not good enough or that you're destined to fail, the RAS will make you more likely to notice situations and feedback that confirm those beliefs. For example, if you're about to give a presentation and you think, "I'm going to mess this up," your brain will hyper-focus on any small misstep or awkward moment, making you feel like a failure. You're less likely to notice positive feedback or moments when things are going well. Over time, this cycle reinforces the belief that you're not capable, which, in turn, reinforces the emotional response of anxiety, stress, or self-doubt.

This is why self-perception is such a powerful force. Your beliefs about yourself create the lens through which you experience the world. They shape your interactions, your responses to challenges, and your emotional state. If you can change your beliefs about yourself, you can fundamentally alter the emotional landscape you operate in.

How Negative Self-Talk Shapes Your Emotions

Negative self-talk is one of the most common ways people undermine their emotional well-being. It's that inner voice that constantly criticizes, doubts, and belittles you. Negative self-talk doesn't just exist in isolation—it directly impacts your emotional state. Every time you engage in this cycle of self-criticism, it sends signals to your brain that reinforce feelings of worthlessness, guilt, and fear. These emotions then affect how you perceive and respond to external situations.

For instance, if you constantly tell yourself that you're not good enough, it's easy to see how this would lead to chronic feelings of **anxiety**, **low self-esteem**, and **self-doubt**. If you're about to face a challenge, you might feel overwhelmed before you even begin because your inner dialogue is telling you that you're not capable of succeeding. This emotional state—rooted in negativity—becomes a **feedback loop**. The more you engage in negative self-talk, the more your brain reinforces those negative feelings, making them more ingrained and harder to break.

The impact of negative self-talk can be particularly damaging in moments of stress or pressure. When you're under pressure, your brain is already in a heightened emotional state, and negative self-talk exacerbates this by reinforcing feelings of inadequacy or failure. This can lead to impulsive decisions, emotional outbursts, or withdrawal. Over time, this pattern of behavior can significantly impact your overall emotional resilience, making it harder to bounce back from setbacks.

Overcoming Negative Self-Talk: How to Change Your Inner Narrative

The good news is that negative self-talk is not a fixed feature of your brain—it can be **changed**. It requires awareness, effort, and a willingness to challenge the thoughts that are holding you back. The key to overcoming negative self-talk is **cognitive reframing**—changing the way you interpret and respond to your thoughts. Cognitive reframing is a process of taking a negative thought and consciously shifting it to a more balanced or constructive perspective.

Here's how you can begin to change your inner narrative:

1. Awareness: Catch the Negative Thoughts

The first step in changing negative self-talk is becoming aware of it. Most people aren't even aware of the constant barrage of negative thoughts running through their heads. They've become so habitual that they almost feel like the truth. To break free from this, you need to train yourself to **catch** these thoughts as they arise. This requires mindfulness and self-awareness.

Start paying attention to your thoughts, especially in moments of stress, frustration, or self-doubt. When you hear yourself thinking, "I'm not good enough," "I always fail," or "I can't do this," take note. Recognizing these thoughts is the first step in taking control of them.

2. Challenge the Negative Thought

Once you've become aware of your negative self-talk, the next step is to challenge it. Ask yourself: "Is this thought really true?" or "Is there evidence that contradicts this belief?" Negative self-talk often exaggerates or distorts reality. When you take a step back and objectively evaluate the situation, you'll often find that the thought is either inaccurate or an overgeneralization.

For example, if you think, "I always mess things up," challenge that by recalling instances where you succeeded. Did you not make progress on a project? Have you received praise for something you've done well? Even if it's a small accomplishment, focus on evidence that contradicts the negative thought. Over time, this will weaken the hold that these thoughts have on you.

3. Reframe the Thought with a Balanced Perspective

Now that you've challenged the negative thought, it's time to reframe it in a way that reflects reality in a more balanced manner. This doesn't mean simply replacing a negative thought with an unrealistic positive one. Instead, aim for a more **balanced** and **constructive** perspective.

For instance, if you think, "I'm terrible at public speaking," reframe it by saying, "I've had challenges with public speaking in the past, but I've made progress, and I'm capable of improving with practice." This reframing doesn't ignore your challenges but puts them in perspective. It acknowledges the possibility of growth and change.

4. Practice Self-Compassion

Changing your inner narrative also involves practicing **self-compassion**. Be kind to yourself, especially when you make mistakes. Negative self-talk often stems from a lack of compassion, where you view yourself as a failure rather than someone who is learning and growing. When you're kind to yourself, you reduce the intensity of negative emotions like shame, guilt, or frustration.

Instead of harshly criticizing yourself, treat yourself the way you would treat a friend—offering understanding and support. By cultivating self-compassion, you reduce the emotional charge of negative self-talk and replace it with a more nurturing and encouraging voice.

Strengthening Positive Self-Awareness to Increase Emotional Resilience

While overcoming negative self-talk is crucial, it's equally important to **strengthen positive self-awareness**—the ability to recognize your strengths, achievements, and potential. Positive self-awareness helps you build emotional resilience by reinforcing the belief that you are capable of handling challenges and adversity.

Here are some strategies to build positive self-awareness:

1. Reflect on Your Strengths and Successes

Take time regularly to reflect on your strengths and accomplishments. This could be through journaling or simply taking a moment each day to acknowledge something you've done well. It could be a small win, like successfully handling a difficult conversation, or a larger achievement, like completing a project at work.

By actively reminding yourself of your successes, you build a **positive self-image** that helps you approach challenges with confidence and resilience. When setbacks occur, you'll be better able to see them as temporary obstacles rather than permanent failures.

2. Practice Gratitude

Gratitude is a powerful tool for shifting your focus away from negativity and toward the positive aspects of your life. Regularly practicing gratitude helps reinforce a sense of abundance and well-being, which fosters a more positive emotional state. This is important because when you're grateful for what you have, you're less likely to be overwhelmed by negative emotions like fear or frustration.

Try keeping a gratitude journal, where you write down three things you're thankful for each day. This simple practice can help shift your mindset from one of lack and scarcity to one of abundance and appreciation.

3. Cultivate a Growth Mindset

A growth mindset—the belief that abilities and intelligence can be developed through effort and learning—helps reinforce a more **resilient** and **positive self-awareness**. When you adopt a growth mindset, you stop seeing failures as reflections of your worth and start viewing them as opportunities for growth.

To cultivate a growth mindset, embrace challenges, seek feedback, and see setbacks as learning experiences rather than signs of inadequacy. By doing so, you reinforce the belief that you can improve, adapt, and grow from any situation.

The Mirror Effect and Emotional Resilience

The way you perceive yourself has a profound impact on your emotional landscape. By changing your self-talk, challenging negative beliefs, and cultivating a more positive self-awareness, you can shift your emotional state from one of reactivity to one of resilience. The brain will reinforce whatever beliefs you hold about yourself, so it's crucial to make those beliefs constructive, empowering, and aligned with your true potential.

The Mirror Effect shows us that by changing the way we view ourselves, we can transform our emotional experiences. When you replace negative self-talk with positive, balanced thoughts and develop self-awareness rooted in growth, you build the emotional resilience needed to face any challenge. Your perception shapes your emotions—so make sure the reflection you see in the mirror is one that supports your emotional well-being.

Chapter 4: The Role of Social Influence in Emotional Control

The Social Brain: How Others Control Your Emotions Without You Knowing

Emotions are not just personal—they're deeply influenced by the people around us. Your mood, behavior, and even your decisions can be shaped by others without you even realizing it. This happens because your brain is wired to be highly sensitive to social cues. We're social creatures by nature, and our survival has always depended on our ability to connect, communicate, and react to those around us. But this also means that, whether you like it or not, the people around you can have a profound impact on your emotions. This concept is referred to as **emotional contagion**—the tendency for one person's emotions to influence the emotions of others in their social circle.

We'll explore the **neural basis** behind social influence and emotional contagion, examining how group dynamics can manipulate your emotional state. We'll also look at how you can protect yourself from toxic emotional environments, and develop strategies to **maintain emotional autonomy** even in the face of external pressure.

The Neural Basis of Social Influence and Emotional Contagion

The brain is a remarkably social organ, designed to connect with others, understand emotions, and react to social stimuli. One of the key systems that facilitate this is the **mirror neuron system**. Mirror neurons are specialized cells in the brain that fire when we perform an action, as well as when we observe someone else performing the same action. These neurons are believed to be crucial for understanding and mimicking the emotions, intentions, and behaviors of others. This system enables us to feel empathy and engage in social interactions, but it also makes us highly susceptible to the emotions of those around us.

When you observe someone feeling happy, sad, or angry, your brain processes their emotional state through these mirror neurons, triggering similar feelings within you. This is why when someone around you is upset, you might feel stressed, anxious, or even depressed. Similarly, when you're in the presence of someone who is calm or positive, their emotional state can uplift yours, even if you weren't initially in a good mood.

This phenomenon is not just about passive observation; the mirror neuron system also allows us to mimic emotional expressions, which can influence how we feel. For example, if you're sitting in a room with people laughing, your brain may trigger laughter in response, even if you initially didn't find the situation funny. This type of **emotional contagion** happens in subtle and automatic ways, and it's part of our innate social wiring.

The Power of Group Dynamics

Humans are highly influenced by the dynamics of the groups they belong to. Whether it's a family, a workplace, or a social circle, group dynamics have a powerful effect on individual emotions. The emotions of a group can be contagious, and often, individuals will align their emotional states with the majority of the group, even if that means suppressing their own feelings or adopting emotions that are not truly theirs.

This influence occurs through **social conformity**—the tendency to adjust one's behavior, attitudes, or beliefs to align with those of a group. It's an evolutionary trait that helped our ancestors stay in harmony with the group and avoid conflicts that could jeopardize survival. In modern society, this behavior still persists, often subconsciously.

For example, when you enter a meeting with a group of people who are visibly tense or frustrated, it's likely that you will also start feeling stressed, even if the subject at hand doesn't directly concern you. You might start to mirror their body language or adopt their emotional state, even if you initially had a different emotional reaction. Similarly, when you're in a group that is excited or happy, your emotional state is likely to shift in that direction as well.

Emotional Contagion in Practice

One of the most common forms of emotional contagion occurs through **facial expressions**. Research has shown that people are very skilled at recognizing and mimicking emotional expressions, even without conscious awareness. For instance, if someone in your group starts frowning or looks upset, your brain automatically picks up on their facial expression and, in turn, you might begin to feel the same way. This automatic response is so ingrained that you may not even realize it's happening. Your emotional state has just been hijacked by someone else's.

But it's not just facial expressions—body language, tone of voice, and even the emotional energy someone else exudes can affect you. If someone enters a room with a positive, enthusiastic attitude, their energy can uplift the group and shift the emotional tone of the room. Conversely, if someone walks in with a negative, cynical attitude, it can bring the overall mood down, affecting everyone's emotional state.

In group settings, whether in the workplace, at home, or among friends, **emotional synchronization** can take place. This is when a group of people aligns their emotional states, consciously or unconsciously. The group's mood becomes the collective emotional state, and individuals often adopt that emotional state without thinking about it. This is why you might leave a meeting feeling exhausted or drained, even if the discussion didn't directly concern you. The emotional atmosphere in the room can take a toll, and you might find yourself emotionally depleted.

Tactics to Protect Yourself from Toxic Emotional Environments

Now that we understand how social dynamics and emotional contagion work, it's important to explore ways to protect yourself from toxic emotional environments and maintain control over your own emotional state. It's easy to get swept away by the emotions of others, but developing emotional **awareness** and **self-regulation** is the key to maintaining balance.

Here are some practical tactics to help you stay emotionally independent:

1. Cultivate Emotional Awareness

The first step in protecting yourself from emotional contagion is to **recognize when your emotions are being influenced by others**. Pay attention to how you feel in different social situations. Do you leave certain interactions feeling drained, frustrated, or anxious? Are there specific people or groups who tend to trigger negative emotional reactions in you? Identifying these triggers is the first step in defending yourself against emotional manipulation.

Once you become aware of how others affect your emotions, you can begin to practice mindfulness in those situations. By observing your emotional state without judgment, you can create space between the external stimulus and your emotional response. This distance allows you to choose how you want to react, rather than being swept away by the emotions of those around you.

2. Set Emotional Boundaries

Setting emotional boundaries is crucial for maintaining emotional autonomy. Emotional boundaries are the limits you set with others to protect your emotional energy. In toxic environments, people may try to draw you into their emotional dramas, but by setting clear emotional boundaries, you can preserve your own emotional stability.

This might mean saying no to conversations that drain you, distancing yourself from people who regularly bring negativity into your life, or simply removing yourself from situations where you feel emotionally overwhelmed. It's important to remember that setting boundaries isn't about being cold or dismissive—it's about **protecting your emotional well-being** so that you can engage with others in a healthy and balanced way.

3. Practice Emotional Detachment

In social environments, especially in emotionally charged situations, it's important to practice **emotional detachment**. This doesn't mean completely shutting yourself off from others, but rather maintaining a sense of emotional distance and not getting overly involved in other people's emotions. By detaching emotionally, you prevent the other person's emotional state from taking over your own.

For example, if someone is angry or upset, you can acknowledge their emotions without taking them on as your own. You can listen and empathize without allowing their frustration to fuel your own anxiety or irritation. One way to practice detachment is to observe the emotions of others as if you were an outsider, without judgment or attachment. This allows you to maintain a sense of emotional balance and not be overwhelmed by external emotional energy.

4. Control Your Environment

If you find that certain people or environments consistently trigger negative emotional responses, it might be time to take control of your surroundings. You have the power to choose where you spend your time and who you engage with. By deliberately placing yourself in environments that support your emotional well-being, you can limit the impact of toxic emotions.

This might mean limiting contact with negative or emotionally draining individuals, avoiding environments that make you feel stressed or anxious, or seeking out people who lift you up and bring positivity into your life. You don't need to tolerate toxic emotional environments—by controlling your environment, you can protect your emotional health.

5. Develop Emotional Resilience

Building emotional resilience is essential for withstanding the emotional turbulence of social environments. Emotional resilience is the ability to bounce back from negative emotions and maintain a sense of stability, even in difficult situations. You can strengthen your emotional resilience by practicing self-care, maintaining a strong support network, and learning emotional regulation techniques.

One key to emotional resilience is to **reframe negative emotional experiences**. Instead of letting someone else's negativity dictate your emotional state, view the situation as an opportunity to practice emotional control. Remind yourself that you are not defined by the emotions of others, and that you have the power to decide how you respond.

Mastering Emotional Independence

The people around you have the power to influence your emotions in subtle and powerful ways. However, with awareness, boundaries, and emotional resilience, you can protect yourself from toxic emotional environments and maintain control over your own emotional state. By cultivating self-awareness, setting clear boundaries, and practicing emotional detachment, you can prevent others from hijacking your emotions. You can control how you feel, regardless of the emotional dynamics at play. Emotional independence is not about isolation; it's about having the strength to protect your emotional well-being while still engaging with the world around you.

Empathy or Exploitation? Navigating Social Interactions to Preserve Your Emotional Integrity

Empathy is often hailed as a virtue. It's the ability to understand and share the feelings of others, and it's one of the fundamental elements of social connection. At its best, empathy allows us to form deep relationships, offer support, and build trust. But what happens when empathy crosses a line? When, instead of strengthening a relationship, it leaves you vulnerable to emotional exploitation?

Understanding the fine line between genuine empathy and manipulation is essential for maintaining emotional integrity in social settings. The truth is, empathy is a double-edged sword. While it can be a powerful tool for connection, it can also be used against you if you're not careful. In this subchapter, we will dive into the **neuroscience of empathy**, explore how it can both help and harm you, and provide you with practical strategies to preserve your emotional integrity in social interactions.

The Neuroscience of Empathy: How Your Brain Reacts to Others' Emotions

Empathy is a complex emotional response that involves multiple areas of the brain. When you experience empathy, your brain activates in ways that are similar to when you are experiencing the emotion yourself. This phenomenon is driven by the **mirror neuron system**, which allows you to "mirror" the emotions and actions of others, essentially putting yourself in their shoes. In this way, you can feel someone else's pain, joy, or frustration.

Research has shown that the brain's **insula**, an area responsible for emotional processing, and the **anterior cingulate cortex**, which is involved in decision-making and emotional regulation, are both activated when you experience empathy. When you see someone in distress, these brain areas prompt you to feel concern for that person, which can drive you to help or comfort them.

However, the same mechanisms that make empathy so powerful can also make you vulnerable. Because your brain automatically mirrors the emotions of others, it can be difficult to discern whether those emotions are truly yours or if you're simply reflecting someone else's emotional state. When empathy becomes overwhelming, your ability to maintain emotional boundaries weakens. In such cases, you may start to prioritize the needs of others over your own, becoming emotionally drained or manipulated.

When Empathy Helps: Building Meaningful Connections

Genuine empathy strengthens social bonds and enhances cooperation. It allows you to understand another person's perspective, which is crucial for building trust and effective communication. When you feel for someone and they feel understood, it opens the door for deeper relationships and emotional closeness. In this way, empathy fosters **emotional reciprocity**, where both parties benefit from the exchange.

For example, in close friendships or romantic relationships, empathy allows partners to support each other during tough times. It helps to ease emotional burdens by offering a safe space for vulnerability. The simple act of listening, showing compassion, and offering understanding can heal emotional wounds and create stronger ties between individuals.

Moreover, empathy is a vital component of effective leadership. Leaders who can empathize with their team members' concerns and aspirations are better able to inspire loyalty and motivate others. When a leader recognizes the emotional states of those they lead, they can provide tailored support and feedback, fostering a work environment that feels safe and supportive. This leads to better collaboration, improved performance, and higher job satisfaction.

When Empathy Hurts: Emotional Contagion and Overwhelm

Despite its benefits, empathy can be **emotionally taxing**. This is particularly true when you absorb the negative emotions of others without the proper boundaries. When someone else's distress triggers your own emotional response, it can lead to **emotional contagion**, where you unintentionally adopt their negative emotional state.

For instance, if a colleague comes to you in a state of anger or frustration, you might begin to feel irritated or upset, even if you initially had no reason to feel that way. This happens because your brain automatically mirrors the emotional state of others, and without awareness or control, you may get caught up in their emotional turmoil.

In such cases, empathy can turn into **emotional overwhelm**, where your capacity to empathize starts to deplete your emotional resources. This can lead to burnout, stress, or resentment, especially if you regularly find yourself taking on the emotions of others. Over time, the emotional demands of others can take a toll, and you may start to feel like you're constantly giving without receiving much in return. This is particularly true in situations where others repeatedly lean on you for emotional support without offering the same in return.

Furthermore, without clear boundaries, empathy can **cloud your judgment**. In an attempt to ease someone else's suffering, you may overlook your own needs or dismiss red flags that suggest that the person you're empathizing with is not being truthful or is taking advantage of your emotional investment.

The Dark Side of Empathy: Emotional Manipulation

While empathy can be a gift, it can also be exploited. People who are aware of your empathetic nature can use it to manipulate you emotionally. This happens when someone intentionally seeks to trigger your compassion and understanding in order to get what they want. Whether it's an emotional plea for help, a guilt trip, or simply playing on your sense of responsibility, **manipulation through empathy** is a tactic used to control others.

Emotional manipulators often use your empathy against you by exaggerating their emotions or distress to gain sympathy. For example, someone might pretend to be in crisis, playing the victim, in order to elicit your help, attention, or resources. The manipulator will present themselves as fragile or helpless, which prompts an empathetic response from you. Your natural inclination will be to help, but the manipulator's true intention may be to exploit your compassion for their own gain.

One common form of emotional manipulation is **guilt-tripping**. When someone makes you feel responsible for their emotional state, it can create a sense of obligation to help, even if doing so isn't in your best interest. In this scenario, your empathy is used to control your actions and dictate your emotional response. Over time, this can lead to a cycle of **emotional indebtedness**, where you feel constantly obligated to cater to the emotional needs of others, often at the expense of your own well-being.

How to Protect Yourself from Emotional Manipulation

Recognizing the fine line between empathy and emotional manipulation is key to maintaining emotional integrity. Here are some strategies to help you protect yourself from being exploited in social situations:

1. Set Clear Emotional Boundaries

The first step in protecting yourself from emotional manipulation is to set clear and firm boundaries. This involves recognizing your emotional limits and learning to say no when necessary. Boundaries help you protect your emotional energy and ensure that you're not constantly giving more than you can handle.

When you set boundaries, you create a space where your empathy can thrive without overwhelming you. It's important to remember that **you are not responsible for fixing everyone's problems**. Empathy doesn't require you to take on the emotional burden of others; it only requires that you understand their feelings and offer support where you can. If you feel emotionally drained or manipulated, it's okay to distance yourself or set a limit on how much you can help.

2. Recognize Emotional Manipulation Tactics

One of the most effective ways to protect yourself is by learning to recognize the signs of emotional manipulation. Manipulators often use guilt, fear, or exaggerated emotions to control your actions. They may create a sense of urgency, making you feel like you need to act immediately to help them.

To counter this, take a moment to assess the situation objectively. Ask yourself whether the person is truly in need, or if they are simply using your empathy as a tool for their own gain. If you feel uncertain, give yourself time to process the request and consider the impact on your emotional health before responding.

3. Practice Emotional Detachment

While empathy involves connecting with others emotionally, it's crucial to practice emotional detachment. This doesn't mean shutting off your emotions, but rather learning to **separate** your emotional response from the other person's emotional state. Emotional detachment allows you to **feel empathy without being consumed by it**.

One way to practice emotional detachment is by observing the person's emotions without immediately reacting. Instead of immediately jumping in to help, take a step back and assess the situation. Ask yourself, "Am I reacting to this person's emotions because I truly feel empathy, or am I being manipulated into feeling responsible for their emotional state?" This pause can give you the clarity to make a conscious decision about how to respond.

4. Develop Emotional Resilience

Building emotional resilience is key to maintaining your emotional autonomy in social interactions. Resilience allows you to withstand the emotional pressure of others without losing your sense of self. This involves **strengthening your emotional self-awareness**, practicing self-care, and cultivating a mindset that prioritizes your emotional well-being.

By developing resilience, you will be better able to handle emotionally charged situations without becoming overwhelmed. You'll also be able to recognize when your empathy is being used to manipulate you, and you'll have the tools to protect your emotional energy.

Navigating Social Interactions with Emotional Integrity

Empathy is a powerful tool for connection, but it's important to recognize that it can also be used to manipulate you if you're not careful. Understanding the neuroscience behind empathy, and learning to distinguish between genuine empathy and emotional manipulation, is essential for preserving your emotional integrity in social settings. By setting boundaries, recognizing manipulation tactics, practicing emotional detachment, and developing resilience, you can protect yourself from being exploited while still maintaining meaningful and compassionate relationships. Emotional autonomy is not about disconnecting from others—it's about being able to engage with them while protecting your own emotional well-being.

Building Emotional Immunity: Protecting Your Emotional Energy from the Outside World

Emotions are contagious. Whether you're aware of it or not, the emotional states of people around you influence your own mood, thoughts, and behaviors. This is something you encounter on a daily basis, whether at work, with friends, or even with strangers. When the person next to you is stressed, angry, or upset, their emotional energy can easily seep into your own mind, clouding your judgment and affecting your emotional stability.

Now, imagine if you could block all that out. Imagine if you could walk through the world, unaffected by other people's emotional states. How much more in control of yourself would you be? How much better would you be able to make decisions, stay composed, and avoid unnecessary emotional conflict?

This isn't a hypothetical question—it's entirely possible to **build emotional immunity**, and it starts with understanding how external emotional stressors affect you and how you can rewire your brain to remain unaffected by them. In this subchapter, we'll explore cognitive strategies to protect yourself from the emotional bombardment of the outside world, discuss how to set emotional boundaries, and show you how to strengthen your emotional energy against external forces.

Cognitive Strategies to Shield Yourself from External Emotional Stressors

First, you need to understand how external emotional stressors work. The brain is a powerful emotional receptor. It constantly processes incoming information and responds accordingly, often without you even being consciously aware of it. When you're exposed to a person's negative emotions—whether it's their anger, sadness, or anxiety—your brain interprets those feelings and responds by mirroring them, at least to some extent. This is why you might feel yourself becoming irritable after a conversation with someone who's angry, or anxious after talking to someone who's nervous. These external emotions are affecting you because your brain is constantly **looking for emotional cues** from the environment to understand and relate to the people around you.

But there's a key difference between **reacting to someone else's emotions** and simply being aware of them. The moment you **react**—you absorb that energy, and your emotional state shifts. In that moment, you lose control. However, when you simply observe someone else's mood without allowing it to affect your own state, you remain in control.

One of the most effective cognitive strategies to prevent this emotional transmission is **mental distancing**. This doesn't mean ignoring the person or their feelings, but it means creating an emotional buffer between yourself and them. The goal here is to recognize that **their emotions are not your own**. They may be angry, anxious, or frustrated, but you don't need to mirror those feelings.

Here's how you can do it:

1. **Recognize Emotional Cues Without Reacting**: The first step is recognizing when emotions are being triggered in you. When you feel yourself getting caught up in someone else's emotional state, take a moment to step back mentally. The moment you acknowledge that someone else's mood is affecting you, you create the space you need to control your response.
2. **Reframe the Situation**: When you start to feel emotionally affected by someone else, reframe the situation in your mind. Instead of thinking "I'm angry because they're angry," tell yourself, "They are angry, but that doesn't mean I have to be." You create a psychological distance between their emotional state and your own by labeling their feelings as theirs, and not allowing them to blend with yours.
3. **Practice Cognitive Defusion**: Cognitive defusion is a technique that involves separating yourself from your thoughts and emotions. When you feel yourself reacting to someone's mood, remind yourself that "I am having the thought that I should feel upset, but that thought doesn't define me." This allows you to notice your emotional reactions without letting them dictate your behavior.

These cognitive strategies act as a shield against the external emotional stressors that surround you. By becoming more aware of how you're influenced by others' emotions, you can break the automatic cycle of emotional contagion.

How to Rewire Your Brain to Stay Unaffected by the Moods of Others

The ability to stay unaffected by the emotional states of others isn't just a matter of willpower—it's a skill you can develop by rewiring your brain. Just as your brain learned to mirror emotions automatically, it can also learn to filter out those unnecessary emotional responses. **Neuroplasticity**, the brain's ability to reorganize itself by forming new neural connections, plays a significant role in this process.

To rewire your brain to remain emotionally unaffected by others, you need to engage in consistent practice that trains your brain to **focus inward** rather than on the emotional cues of others. This is where the power of **mindfulness** and **self-regulation** come in. With time, these practices can reshape the neural pathways that respond to external emotional stimuli.

Here's how to rewire your brain for emotional immunity:

1. **Strengthen Your Prefrontal Cortex**: The prefrontal cortex (PFC) is the part of your brain responsible for **decision-making**, **self-control**, and **emotional regulation**. It helps you stay calm under pressure and think rationally, even in emotional situations. The more you exercise your PFC through self-awareness and reflection, the better you will become at controlling your emotional responses to others. Practices like mindfulness meditation and controlled breathing exercises have been shown to strengthen the PFC, helping you become less reactive to external emotional stressors.
2. **Regular Mindfulness Meditation**: Mindfulness meditation trains your brain to observe thoughts and emotions without reacting. By practicing mindfulness regularly, you can train your mind to stay calm and centered, no matter how intense the external emotional stimuli. As you meditate, focus on your breath, and observe your thoughts and feelings as they come and go. With practice, you will develop a greater ability to separate yourself from the emotions of others, making it easier to stay unaffected by external stressors.
3. **Practice Emotional Reappraisal**: Emotional reappraisal is the

process of **changing your emotional response to a situation** by changing how you think about it. When someone expresses anger or frustration, instead of reacting emotionally, reappraise the situation by asking yourself, "What's really going on here? Why is this person upset?" By shifting your perspective, you can remain calm and rational, rather than getting caught up in their emotional energy.

4. **Self-Compassion and Acceptance**: Being emotionally resilient is not about suppressing your emotions or denying their existence. Instead, it's about learning to accept your emotions without being overwhelmed by them. Practice **self-compassion** by treating yourself with the same kindness and understanding that you would offer a friend. By accepting your emotions without judgment, you can prevent them from taking control of your actions and thoughts.

With time and practice, these strategies will help rewire your brain to stay unaffected by the moods of others. The more consistently you apply these techniques, the more your brain will adapt, making it easier to maintain emotional autonomy in any social situation.

The Concept of Emotional Boundaries and How to Set Them Effectively

Emotional boundaries are one of the most important tools you have for protecting your emotional energy. Just as physical boundaries keep your personal space safe from intruders, emotional boundaries protect your emotional energy from being drained by others. Without clear boundaries, you can easily become overwhelmed by other people's emotional needs, expectations, and demands.

Setting emotional boundaries means learning to say "no" when you need to, not taking on the emotions of others, and protecting your inner peace. **Emotional boundaries** allow you to engage with others without compromising your emotional well-being.

Here's how you can set and enforce emotional boundaries effectively:

1. **Know Your Limits**: The first step in setting boundaries is understanding your own emotional limits. This means being clear about what you can and cannot tolerate emotionally. For example, if you know that being around negative or anxious people drains your

energy, you can set a boundary by limiting your exposure to them.

2. **Learn to Say No**: One of the most important skills in setting emotional boundaries is learning to say no. This doesn't mean being rude or rejecting people, but it means being firm about your limits. If someone asks for emotional support that you can't provide, it's okay to politely say no. You can offer your empathy without taking on their emotional burden.
3. **Communicate Your Boundaries Clearly**: It's important to communicate your boundaries clearly and assertively. This might mean telling someone that you're not available to listen to their problems at the moment or letting them know that you need some space to recharge. Clear communication helps others understand your limits, and it reduces the chance of being emotionally manipulated.
4. **Enforce Your Boundaries with Consistency**: Setting boundaries is one thing, but enforcing them is another. Be consistent in applying your boundaries. If you allow others to cross your emotional boundaries once, they may continue to do so. By being consistent and firm, you reinforce your right to protect your emotional energy.
5. **Practice Self-Care**: Emotional boundaries are not just about protecting yourself from others—they're also about protecting yourself from your own internal emotional demands. Take time for self-care activities that help you recharge emotionally, whether that's through exercise, hobbies, or simply taking time to be alone. When you practice self-care, you replenish your emotional reserves and strengthen your ability to maintain boundaries.

Building emotional immunity is not about shutting yourself off from others; it's about learning to protect your emotional energy and stay unaffected by the external emotional chaos around you. By using cognitive strategies like mental distancing, mindfulness, and emotional reappraisal, you can rewire your brain to stay calm and composed in the face of emotional stressors. Additionally, setting clear emotional boundaries is essential for protecting your emotional energy and ensuring that you don't become overwhelmed by the moods of others.

In a world that constantly demands your emotional attention, developing emotional immunity is a powerful tool for maintaining control over your own emotional landscape. When you can protect your emotional energy, you become more resilient, more focused, and more capable of navigating life's challenges with clarity and strength.

Chapter 5: The Hidden Enemies: How Negative Emotions Sabotage Your Life

The Neuroscience of Fear: Breaking the Cycle of Paralysis

Fear is an emotion we all know well. It's universal, primal, and something every person has experienced at some point. Whether it's fear of failure, fear of judgment, or even physical fear, it can grip you, paralyze you, and keep you from acting. Fear is a survival mechanism—its role in evolution is clear: it helps you avoid danger and stay alive. However, in modern times, the same fear response, which was once essential for survival, often triggers unnecessary paralysis in situations that pose no real threat.

But what if you could break this cycle? What if you could take the power of fear and transform it from something that limits you to something that propels you forward? The key is understanding the neuroscience of fear and learning how to desensitize your response, turning fear into a tool rather than a hindrance.

The Brain's Fear Response: Evolutionary Advantages and Modern-Day Dysfunctions

The brain's fear response is wired deep into our biology. It's a mechanism that helped our ancestors survive in an unpredictable and dangerous world. When faced with a threat—whether it was a predator or an enemy—the brain would activate the **amygdala**, which is the part of the brain responsible for detecting threats and generating emotional responses. This quick and automatic response would trigger a "fight or flight" reaction, preparing the body to either confront the danger or escape it.

In evolutionary terms, fear was a life-saving tool. The quick activation of the amygdala ensured that an individual could react swiftly to potential threats. This response would elevate heart rate, increase adrenaline production, and sharpen focus, all while preparing the body to either fight or run.

However, in modern society, many of the threats we encounter are not life-threatening. Fear in today's world is often triggered by social situations, work stress, or personal challenges—none of which require the "fight or flight" response. Yet, our brains continue to react as though we're facing physical danger. This is where the dysfunction comes in. Instead of empowering us to take action, our fear response often causes paralysis, anxiety, and avoidance, especially when the fear is irrational or disproportionate to the actual situation. The **prefrontal cortex**, the area of the brain responsible for higher-level thinking, decision-making, and problem-solving, can sometimes help moderate the amygdala's overreaction. But the more intense the fear response, the harder it is for the prefrontal cortex to keep the amygdala in check. This creates a feedback loop: fear triggers the amygdala, which strengthens the fear response, making it harder to think logically or act decisively. This is the cycle of **paralysis**—the more you fear something, the more it controls you.

Techniques to Desensitize Fear and Turn It Into a Source of Strength

Understanding how fear works on a neurological level is only the beginning. Now you need to learn how to break the cycle and desensitize your fear. The key lies in **exposure** and **reframing.** By gradually confronting your fears in a controlled way and learning how to reframe them, you can retrain your brain to respond differently.

1. **Gradual Exposure: Desensitizing Your Fear Response**

The concept of **gradual exposure** comes from cognitive-behavioral therapy (CBT) and is one of the most effective methods for reducing the intensity of fear. Exposure therapy works by slowly and repeatedly confronting the feared object, situation, or thought, which allows the brain to adjust its response. Over time, the fear becomes less overwhelming, and you gain the ability to handle it with composure.

Here's how gradual exposure works:

- **Start Small**: Begin by identifying a fear that's relatively minor but still causes you discomfort. For example, if you have a fear of public speaking, start by speaking in front of a mirror or recording yourself. The goal here is not to immediately face your biggest fear but to start by engaging with the fear in a manageable way.
- **Increase the Challenge Slowly**: As you get more comfortable,

increase the intensity of your exposure. For example, after practicing in front of a mirror, you might speak in front of a trusted friend or family member. Then, gradually work your way up to a larger audience, until the fear becomes something you can face with relative calm.

- **Repetition**: Repeated exposure is key to desensitization. The more often you confront your fear, the more the brain begins to recognize that there's no real threat. As the brain gets used to the situation, the intensity of the fear response will diminish. This works because the brain learns to associate the feared situation with a neutral or even positive experience.

1. **Reframing Fear: Turning Anxiety Into Action**

Reframing is another essential tool for turning fear into strength. The way you interpret fear can significantly affect how you respond to it. Instead of seeing fear as something paralyzing, you can reframe it as something motivating. Fear is not inherently negative—it's simply a signal from your brain that you care about something or that something important is at stake.
Here's how to reframe your fear response:

- **Label Fear as Excitement**: One of the simplest ways to reframe fear is by **relabeling** it. When you feel fear, tell yourself, "I'm excited." The physical sensations of fear—elevated heart rate, shallow breathing, heightened alertness—are very similar to the physical symptoms of excitement. Instead of viewing these sensations as negative, embrace them as signs that you're preparing for something significant. By consciously choosing to frame your fear as excitement, you can shift your mental state and use the fear to fuel action, not inaction.
- **Focus on Your Goals, Not the Threat**: Fear often arises because you're focused on the potential negative outcomes. The brain is wired to anticipate worst-case scenarios. But by focusing on the potential **positive outcomes** of facing your fear, you can shift your perspective. Ask yourself, "What will I gain if I overcome this fear? How will this improve my life or bring me closer to my goals?" The more you

can focus on your desired outcome, the more you'll reframe the fear response into something productive.

- **Visualize Success**: Visualization is a powerful technique that can help retrain your brain. Before you engage with a feared situation, close your eyes and **visualize** yourself handling the situation calmly and successfully. Imagine yourself walking through the fear and emerging victorious. This doesn't just prepare your mind for success—it also rewires the brain to associate the feared situation with a positive, confident outcome.

1. **Mindfulness: Staying Present with Your Fear**

Mindfulness is a practice that can help you stay grounded in the moment, even when fear arises. When you're feeling fearful, your mind often jumps into the future, imagining worst-case scenarios. This creates anxiety. But mindfulness teaches you to stay present, to observe the fear without getting swept away by it.

Here's how to use mindfulness to manage fear:

- **Observe Without Judgment**: When fear arises, instead of getting caught up in it, try to observe the fear as if it's a passing cloud. Simply notice the physical sensations (tightness in your chest, racing heart, etc.) and the thoughts that come up. Don't label them as "bad" or "negative." Just let them exist without judgment. The more you practice observing your fear without reacting to it, the less power it will have over you.
- **Breathing Techniques**: One of the most effective ways to calm fear is through **controlled breathing**. When you're afraid, your body's fight-or-flight response kicks in, making your breathing shallow and fast. By consciously slowing your breath, you can activate your body's relaxation response, which counteracts the fear. Try inhaling deeply for four seconds, holding the breath for four seconds, and exhaling slowly for four seconds. Repeat this cycle until your heart rate slows and you feel more in control.

- **Body Scan**: Another mindfulness technique is the body scan, which involves mentally scanning your body from head to toe and noticing areas of tension. When fear arises, it often manifests as physical tension. By practicing body scanning, you can identify and release this tension, helping your body return to a calm state.

Practical Exercises for Overcoming Fear-Based Thinking

Now that you have the tools to desensitize your fear and turn it into a source of strength, it's important to put these strategies into practice. Here are a few **exercises** you can use to break free from fear-based thinking:

1. **Fear Journaling**: Take a few minutes each day to write down the specific fears that are holding you back. Write about what scares you, why it scares you, and what you imagine might happen if you face it. Then, challenge each fear by asking, "Is this fear rational? What's the worst that could happen? What's the best that could happen?" Writing these fears down helps to externalize them, making them less powerful and easier to confront.
2. **Fear Exposure Ladder**: Create a list of things that scare you, ranked from least scary to most scary. Start with the least frightening task, such as speaking to a stranger or making a phone call you've been avoiding. Gradually work your way up the ladder to more challenging situations. Each time you face a fear, reflect on how your body and mind respond, and notice how your fear gradually lessens with each exposure.
3. **Reframing Practice**: Practice reframing your fear responses in real-time. Next time you feel afraid, pause for a moment and ask yourself, "How can I reframe this fear into excitement or motivation? What's the opportunity here?" This practice of shifting your mindset helps you turn fear into a driving force rather than an obstacle.

Fear, when left unchecked, can dominate your life. But when you understand the neuroscience behind fear, and learn how to desensitize your response, reframe your thinking, and stay present with your emotions, you take back control. Fear can become a powerful tool that sharpens your focus, drives your actions, and helps you achieve your goals. It's no longer something to avoid or escape—it's a signal that you are alive, that you care, and that you are ready to face the challenge head-on.

The Rage Within: Understanding Anger and How to Neutralize It

Anger is an emotion many people struggle to control. It can feel like a sudden, powerful force that takes over your body and mind, often leading to impulsive reactions that you later regret. Whether it's triggered by an injustice, a personal slight, or simply frustration, anger can be both destructive and exhausting. But beneath the surface of this emotion, there's something more at play—a deep-rooted survival mechanism that evolved to protect us from harm. Understanding why anger exists and how it functions in the brain is the first step to regaining control over it.

The Anatomy of Anger: Why It's a Survival Instinct That Often Misfires

To understand how to neutralize anger, you first need to understand why it happens. Anger, like fear, is an emotion that has evolved over millions of years. It is rooted in the **fight-or-flight** response, a mechanism that prepared our ancestors to deal with immediate threats. When faced with danger, the body needed a way to respond quickly—either by fighting the threat or running from it. Anger is the emotional fuel that powers the "fight" part of that equation.

The brain structures involved in anger are similar to those that handle fear. The **amygdala**, a small almond-shaped cluster of nuclei deep within the brain, plays a central role in processing emotions like fear and anger. When a situation triggers a sense of injustice or threat, the amygdala rapidly processes the information and sends signals to other brain regions to prepare the body for action. In the case of anger, this means activating the sympathetic nervous system, which increases heart rate, raises blood pressure, and floods the body with stress hormones like adrenaline and cortisol.

However, while anger was once a vital survival tool, helping humans defend themselves against predators or threats, it no longer serves the same life-or-death purpose in modern society. Today, the same brain structures that once protected us are being activated by everyday frustrations, misunderstandings, or perceived slights that are, in fact, not life-threatening. The result is a "misfire" of the anger response. It's no longer triggered by real danger but by psychological or emotional stressors, leading to disproportionate reactions.

This is where the problem lies. Anger is a natural emotion, but the way it manifests in modern life often leads to negative consequences. People act out in anger, saying things they don't mean, doing things they later regret, and damaging relationships that are important to them. Understanding the **neurobiology** behind anger can help you recognize when it's about to take hold and give you the tools to short-circuit it before it gets out of hand.

How to Short-Circuit Rage Before It Takes Hold

Anger, when it strikes, often feels uncontrollable. The body and mind are flooded with overwhelming emotions and physical sensations that seem to take over your ability to think clearly or act rationally. But the truth is, you can control this process if you act early enough. Recognizing the signs of anger as they appear and intervening before they escalate is key to mastering it.

1. **Recognize the Warning Signs**

The first step to controlling anger is learning to **recognize** the early signs before they become full-blown rage. Anger doesn't always explode suddenly; it often starts small, with subtle physical and emotional cues. These can include:

- **Increased tension in your body**, especially in the jaw, shoulders, or fists.
- **A racing heartbeat** or shallow breathing.
- **A sense of irritation** or frustration that gradually builds.
- **Negative thoughts** or a desire to blame others.

By becoming aware of these signals, you can intervene before the anger becomes overwhelming. Awareness is the key to breaking the cycle of rage.

1. **The Pause Technique: Creating Space Between Stimulus and Reaction**

Once you notice these early warning signs, you need to **pause**. The brain's reaction to anger is immediate—it's an automatic process that happens before your conscious mind can even evaluate the situation. This is the power of the amygdala's response: it acts quickly to prepare the body to act, often before you've had a chance to think.

But with practice, you can learn to slow down this process. By taking a **brief pause**—a few seconds to breathe deeply, count to ten, or simply step away from the situation—you create space between the stimulus (the event that triggered the anger) and your reaction. This allows your prefrontal cortex, the brain's decision-making center, to step in and moderate the emotional response. The pause is the key to disrupting the automatic, impulsive reaction to anger.

The more you practice pausing in moments of anger, the easier it becomes to **interrupt the cycle**. With enough practice, this brief pause can become a habit that you use automatically when anger arises, giving you the time to assess the situation calmly and make a rational decision.

1. **Breathing Techniques to Calm Your Nervous System**

Breathing is one of the most effective tools you have for managing anger. When you're angry, your body is flooded with stress hormones, and your heart rate increases. This physical arousal can make it feel impossible to think straight. Deep, slow breathing has been shown to **activate the parasympathetic nervous system**, which is the body's natural "rest and digest" response. This counteracts the fight-or-flight reaction and helps bring the body back to a state of calm.

Here's a simple breathing technique to use when you feel anger rising:

- **Breathe in slowly through your nose** for a count of four.
- **Hold your breath for a count of four**.
- **Exhale slowly through your mouth** for a count of six.

This technique works by slowing down your breathing, which in turn slows your heart rate and signals to your brain that there's no immediate threat. With enough practice, this breathing technique can become an automatic response to anger, helping you regain control when you need it most.

1. Cognitive Reframing: Changing Your Thoughts to Change Your Emotions

Anger is often fueled by our **thoughts**—the beliefs and assumptions we hold about the world, ourselves, and others. When something triggers our anger, we often jump to conclusions or make negative assumptions about the situation. For example, you might think, "That person is disrespecting me" or "This is unfair, and I can't let it slide." These thoughts create an emotional reaction, which then drives the physical sensations of anger.

One way to short-circuit anger is through **cognitive reframing**—the process of changing the way you interpret a situation. Instead of focusing on the injustice or unfairness of the situation, try to look at it from a different angle. Ask yourself questions like:

- "Is there another explanation for this behavior?"
- "What's the worst that could happen if I stay calm?"
- "How important is this really in the grand scheme of things?"

By changing the way you think about the situation, you can change the emotional response that follows. Cognitive reframing can help you see things from a more balanced, less reactive perspective, reducing the intensity of your anger.

Anger Management Techniques Based on Neurobiology and Mindfulness

In addition to the techniques mentioned above, there are other strategies rooted in neurobiology and mindfulness that can help you manage and neutralize anger.

1. Mindfulness Meditation: Observing Without Judgment

Mindfulness meditation is a practice that helps you observe your emotions without getting caught up in them. When you feel anger rising, instead of fighting it or trying to suppress it, mindfulness teaches you to **observe** the emotion from a distance, without judgment. You become aware of the sensation of anger in your body—how it feels, where it manifests, and what thoughts are accompanying it—without allowing yourself to act on it.

Mindfulness meditation has been shown to **reduce the intensity of emotional responses** by training the brain to become more aware of its automatic reactions. Studies have found that individuals who regularly practice mindfulness experience lower levels of emotional reactivity and greater emotional resilience.

To practice mindfulness when you feel anger, take a moment to:

- **Focus on your breath** and bring your attention to the present moment.
- **Notice the physical sensations** of anger in your body (tension, heat, tightness).
- **Acknowledge the emotion** without judgment or the urge to act on it.

By practicing mindfulness, you create a space between feeling angry and acting on it, allowing you to make a more measured response.

1. The Power of Forgiveness: Releasing Resentment

One of the most powerful ways to neutralize anger is to practice **forgiveness.** Holding onto grudges or harboring resentment only keeps anger alive in your body. When you forgive, you release the emotional charge associated with the situation. This doesn't mean condoning the other person's behavior, but it means letting go of the emotional hold it has over you.

Forgiveness is a process, and it can take time. However, research shows that forgiveness can **lower stress hormones** like cortisol and promote a sense of emotional well-being. By releasing anger through forgiveness, you not only improve your emotional health but also free yourself from the cycle of rage.

Anger is an emotion that, while deeply rooted in our biology, can be managed and controlled with the right strategies. Understanding the neurobiology of anger helps you recognize when it's happening and gives you the tools to intervene early. By using techniques like the pause, deep breathing, cognitive reframing, mindfulness, and forgiveness, you can short-circuit rage before it takes over.

Anger doesn't have to control you. With awareness and practice, you can learn to neutralize it, turning it from a destructive force into an opportunity for emotional growth. By mastering your anger, you take back control of your emotional landscape and increase your ability to handle difficult situations with calm and clarity.

The Weight of Guilt and Shame: Releasing Yourself from Self-Imposed Prison

Guilt and shame are among the most powerful emotions that people carry, often without even realizing the extent of their impact. They can feel like an invisible weight on your chest, a constant reminder of past mistakes, or something you've done—or failed to do—that causes you to feel unworthy, broken, or less than others. Guilt and shame are pervasive, and in many cases, they are self-inflicted. They often become habitual, so ingrained in your psyche that they're not even recognized as emotions anymore—they're just part of who you are. But the truth is, carrying guilt and shame does far more damage than most people realize. These emotions not only affect your mental well-being but also deeply impact your body and brain.

Before we explore how to break free from these emotions, it's important to understand why they exist, how they affect you, and what they're really doing to your mind and body. Only by recognizing the destructive nature of guilt and shame can you begin to break the chains that bind you and take steps toward emotional freedom.

The Chemical Impact of Guilt and Shame on Your Brain and Body

To understand how guilt and shame influence your emotional state, you must first understand their **chemical** and **neurological** effects. These two emotions are not just thoughts—they have physical manifestations that impact your brain's function and your body's physiological state.

Guilt, often linked to the idea of "I did something wrong," and shame, related to "I am wrong," both activate the **amygdala**, the brain's emotion-processing center, and initiate the body's stress response. When these emotions are triggered, your body begins to flood with stress hormones, particularly **cortisol** and **adrenaline**. These chemicals are part of the body's "fight-or-flight" response, and they prepare you for action by increasing heart rate, tightening muscles, and heightening your senses. However, when guilt and shame are persistent, these reactions become harmful because the body stays in a constant state of arousal, unable to return to a balanced, calm state. This prolonged state of stress is linked to numerous health issues, including **chronic anxiety**, **insomnia**, **digestive problems**, and **cardiovascular issues**.

In addition to cortisol, **oxytocin**—a hormone associated with feelings of connection and safety—is often suppressed when guilt and shame dominate the emotional landscape. High levels of guilt and shame can lead to a reduction in oxytocin, which makes it harder for you to feel a sense of belonging or comfort. You may find yourself withdrawing from others or avoiding close relationships because of the negative self-perception these emotions reinforce.

Shame, in particular, can be incredibly isolating. It often triggers a **neural feedback loop** that reinforces the feeling of being inherently flawed or unworthy. This internalized belief becomes a self-fulfilling prophecy: the more shame you feel, the more you engage in behaviors that reinforce that sense of inadequacy. You avoid seeking help or connecting with others because you believe they will see you as unworthy or broken.

Why Guilt and Shame Are So Destructive to Your Emotional Well-Being

Guilt and shame are powerful because they can quickly take root in your core sense of self. They do not only target specific actions or events—they often define your **identity**. When you feel guilty, it's typically because you've done something you believe is wrong. But when you feel shame, it's often because you believe there is something inherently wrong with you, that you are fundamentally flawed, or that you are unworthy of acceptance or love. This can create a **vicious cycle** that spirals deeper and deeper into self-criticism and self-punishment.

Unlike other emotions, such as anger or frustration, which can be more straightforward and transient, guilt and shame are harder to escape from. They are often linked to deep-rooted beliefs about who you are as a person and what you deserve. This makes them particularly **destructive** because they undermine your sense of self-worth and can lead to long-term emotional pain.

One of the reasons guilt and shame are so toxic is that they often make you feel as though **there's no way out**. When you feel guilty, you may believe you can never truly atone for your mistake, or that the damage is irreversible. When you feel shame, you may believe that you're unworthy of love or forgiveness, creating a deep-seated belief that you are doomed to fail and unworthy of growth.

From a neurological perspective, guilt and shame are **emotionally taxing**. They drain your mental and emotional energy, making it difficult to focus on positive goals, take healthy risks, or experience joy. The emotional energy spent on maintaining these feelings can leave you with little capacity to nurture your emotional resilience or cultivate self-compassion.

Psychologically, guilt and shame also keep you trapped in the past. Instead of being able to focus on the present moment and move forward, you remain anchored to the mistakes you've made or the perceived flaws you believe define you. This makes it nearly impossible to heal and grow, as your sense of self is constantly filtered through the lens of guilt or shame.

Steps to Break Free from Guilt and Shame through Self-Forgiveness and Reprocessing

The path to emotional freedom begins with **awareness**. You cannot break free from guilt and shame if you do not first recognize how they are affecting you. Once you understand their impact on your brain and body, the next step is to **process** these emotions in a healthy, constructive way. This is where **self-forgiveness** and **reprocessing** come into play.

1. **Reframe Your Perception of Guilt and Shame**

The first step to overcoming guilt and shame is to **reframe** the way you perceive these emotions. Instead of seeing them as signs of a flawed character or as irremediable states, view them as **signals**—clues to areas in your life where you may need growth or change.

Guilt, for example, can be seen as an opportunity for **growth and correction**. It signals that you've acted in a way that doesn't align with your values or the person you want to be. The key to processing guilt is to understand that it doesn't define your entire being—it's just a temporary emotional response that highlights an area of potential improvement. Similarly, shame doesn't have to define your identity. It's an emotion tied to an action or event, not an inherent flaw within you.

By reframing guilt and shame as **temporary emotional experiences** rather than permanent aspects of who you are, you begin the process of distancing yourself from these emotions. This distance allows you to examine them more objectively and process them in a healthier way.

1. **Engage in Self-Forgiveness**

The act of **self-forgiveness** is critical in breaking free from the cycle of guilt and shame. It's easy to feel that, in order to move on from something, you need to make up for the wrong you've done or be punished for your actions. But self-forgiveness doesn't mean excusing bad behavior—it means accepting that you are **human**, that mistakes are part of life, and that you have the power to learn from those mistakes and grow.

To practice self-forgiveness, begin by acknowledging the mistake or situation that triggered your guilt or shame. Then, ask yourself:

- **What can I learn from this?**
- **How can I avoid making this same mistake in the future?**
- **What steps can I take to make amends or correct my actions?**

By framing the situation as an opportunity for learning and growth, rather than as a source of permanent shame, you shift your focus away from punishment and toward **healing**. You can forgive yourself by acknowledging that the mistake does not define your character, and that it is something you can learn from, not something to hold against yourself forever.

1. **Reprocessing Guilt and Shame Through Mindfulness**

Mindfulness is a powerful tool for processing guilt and shame. By practicing mindfulness, you create the space to observe these emotions without getting caught up in them. Instead of letting guilt or shame take hold of you and dictate your behavior, mindfulness allows you to **witness** these emotions with curiosity, without judgment.

One mindfulness practice you can use to release guilt and shame is the **loving-kindness meditation**. This practice involves sending compassion and forgiveness to yourself and others. It's particularly useful for **breaking down** the walls that guilt and shame build around your heart.

Start by focusing on your breath, and then silently repeat phrases like:

- "May I be happy."
- "May I be healthy."
- "May I live with ease."

Gradually, expand these wishes to others in your life, including those you may have wronged or who have wronged you. By cultivating a sense of **compassion**, you can neutralize the negative energy of guilt and shame, replacing it with self-acceptance and love.

1. **Create New Habits of Self-Compassion**

One of the most effective ways to break free from guilt and shame is by **practicing self-compassion** on a regular basis. This involves being kind and understanding toward yourself, especially when you make mistakes. Treat yourself with the same care, patience, and understanding that you would offer a close friend.

Self-compassion helps you build a positive **self-image** and reduces the hold that guilt and shame have on your sense of self. Instead of being your own harshest critic, practice being your own best friend, offering support and encouragement when things go wrong.

Guilt and shame are powerful emotions, but they do not define you. They are temporary responses to specific actions, and they can be processed and released. By understanding their chemical impact on your brain and body, reframing their meaning, and using techniques like self-forgiveness, mindfulness, and self-compassion, you can break free from the weight of guilt and shame. Through this process, you reclaim your emotional freedom, and you empower yourself to move forward with a renewed sense of self-worth and emotional strength.

Chapter 6: Cultivating Emotional Freedom: A New Way of Living

The Neurobiology of Positivity: Building a Resilient Emotional State

Positive emotions are far more than just fleeting moments of happiness. In fact, they have a profound effect on your brain and emotional well-being. Unlike negative emotions, which tend to trigger automatic, defensive reactions, positive emotions can reshape your brain's neural architecture, helping you develop a more resilient emotional state. Over time, this rewiring doesn't just make you feel better in the short term—it actually creates long-lasting changes that make you better equipped to handle the stress, pressure, and challenges that life throws your way.

But the real question is: How do you build a more resilient emotional state? How do you create lasting changes in your emotional patterns and cultivate positive emotions more consistently? The answer lies in understanding how the brain works and then intentionally practicing habits that foster a positive emotional environment.

How Positive Emotions Reshape the Brain and Build Resilience

The brain is an incredibly adaptive organ. It's built to respond to experiences and adjust based on the environments we encounter. The more you experience a certain type of emotion, the more your brain strengthens the neural pathways that produce that emotion. This is known as **neuroplasticity**—the brain's ability to reorganize itself and form new neural connections in response to experience.

Positive emotions like **joy**, **gratitude**, and **hope** activate specific regions in the brain, and these regions are not just responsible for the immediate feeling of pleasure or contentment; they also play a crucial role in building emotional resilience over time.

One of the most important brain regions involved in positive emotions is the **prefrontal cortex**. The prefrontal cortex is responsible for higher-level thinking, decision-making, and emotional regulation. It's the part of the brain that helps you control impulsive reactions, think critically, and plan for the future. When positive emotions are activated, the prefrontal cortex is strengthened, which, in turn, improves your ability to regulate emotions, solve problems, and handle stress effectively. This means that by regularly cultivating positive emotions, you're actually **training** your brain to become more resilient in the face of adversity.

In contrast, negative emotions like fear, anger, or sadness tend to engage the **amygdala**, which is responsible for processing threats and emotions tied to survival. When you experience negative emotions, the amygdala triggers the fight-or-flight response, activating the body's stress systems and heightening your emotional reactivity. While these responses can be useful in life-threatening situations, they can also be counterproductive when the threat is more abstract or manageable—like stress at work or an argument with a friend.

The more you experience negative emotions, the more your brain becomes wired to respond with defensiveness, anxiety, or anger. But the opposite is also true. When you regularly practice cultivating positive emotions, you help activate the **reward systems** in the brain, including the **dopaminergic system** and the **mesolimbic pathway**, which are responsible for feelings of pleasure, motivation, and satisfaction. This creates a feedback loop of positivity that not only makes you feel better but also improves your ability to handle stress and adversity.

This process of rewiring your brain to embrace positive emotions doesn't happen overnight, but the more you practice it, the stronger and more resilient your emotional state becomes.

Practical Tools for Cultivating Joy, Gratitude, and Hope on a Daily Basis

Building a resilient emotional state takes effort and consistency. It requires intentional practice. Fortunately, there are simple, actionable tools that you can incorporate into your daily life to strengthen positive emotions like joy, gratitude, and hope.

1. Gratitude Practice

Gratitude is one of the most powerful emotions when it comes to building resilience. It's not just about being thankful for big, life-changing moments, but also appreciating the small, everyday things that often go unnoticed. Research shows that people who regularly practice gratitude experience lower levels of stress, anxiety, and depression, while also having better overall emotional well-being.

To cultivate gratitude, start by keeping a **gratitude journal**. Every day, write down three things you're thankful for. These can be big things—like your health or a supportive friend—or small things—like a good cup of coffee in the morning or a beautiful sunset. The key is to consistently find things to appreciate, no matter how small they might seem. Over time, this practice trains your brain to focus on the positive aspects of life, rather than automatically honing in on what's wrong or what's missing.

You can also practice **gratitude in the moment** by taking time throughout the day to consciously notice and appreciate what's around you. This can be as simple as pausing for a few seconds to appreciate a nice conversation with a colleague or feeling grateful for a moment of quiet after a busy day. The more you train yourself to find gratitude in your daily life, the more natural it becomes—and the stronger your emotional resilience will be.

2. Joyful Experiences

Another way to build resilience through positive emotions is by intentionally creating and seeking out experiences that bring you joy. **Joy** is a powerful emotion because it activates the brain's reward systems, releasing **dopamine** and **endorphins**, which are chemicals that make you feel happy, motivated, and energized.

To cultivate joy, start by identifying activities or experiences that consistently bring you happiness. These don't have to be grand gestures or expensive outings; often, the simplest things bring the most joy. For example, it could be listening to your favorite song, going for a walk in nature, playing a game with friends, or engaging in a creative activity like painting or writing.

The goal is to incorporate small doses of joy into your daily routine. Instead of waiting for joy to come to you, take **intentional action** to create it. Schedule time for activities that make you feel good and embrace those moments fully. By making joy a priority in your life, you start to rewire your brain to seek out positive experiences, which increases your overall sense of well-being.

3. Hope and Optimism

Hope is another emotion that has a profound impact on emotional resilience. It's the belief that things can get better, that challenges can be overcome, and that there is a possibility for growth and change. Hope is tied to the **prefrontal cortex**, the area of the brain that allows you to plan and set goals. When you focus on hopeful thoughts, you engage your prefrontal cortex, which strengthens your ability to navigate difficulties and stay motivated in the face of adversity.

To cultivate hope, start by setting small, achievable goals that are aligned with your values. These goals don't have to be monumental—they simply need to be meaningful and give you a sense of purpose. Break down larger, long-term goals into smaller steps that feel attainable. When you achieve even the smallest goal, take time to celebrate your success and reinforce the belief that you can overcome challenges.

Another powerful way to nurture hope is through **positive self-talk**. The way you speak to yourself influences your brain's perception of possibility. Instead of focusing on what's not working or what could go wrong, practice shifting your inner dialogue toward positive and hopeful statements. For example, instead of saying, "This is too hard, I'll never be able to do it," try saying, "This may be difficult, but I can handle it and keep moving forward." Over time, this shift in mindset can dramatically change your outlook on life.

4. Mindfulness and Positive Emotions

Mindfulness is another tool that can help you cultivate positive emotions. When you practice mindfulness, you bring your attention fully to the present moment without judgment. This practice can significantly improve your emotional state by reducing rumination (which often leads to negative emotions like anxiety, guilt, or sadness) and fostering a deeper appreciation for the present.

Mindfulness also helps you become more aware of your thoughts, allowing you to challenge negative thought patterns and replace them with more positive ones. For example, when you catch yourself thinking something like, "I'll never get this right," mindfulness can help you pause, notice the thought, and then shift it to something more optimistic, such as, "I may not have it perfect right now, but I'm making progress, and that's what matters."

You can practice mindfulness through simple techniques like deep breathing, body scans, or mindful observation of your surroundings. Just a few minutes of mindfulness each day can significantly improve your ability to regulate your emotions and cultivate positivity.

Using the Power of Positivity to Rewire Your Emotional Responses Permanently

The more consistently you engage in practices that cultivate positive emotions, the more your brain becomes wired for **resilience**. When positive emotions are regularly activated, they help reduce the impact of negative emotions. Over time, you'll find that you're more able to handle stress without being overwhelmed by it, more able to recover from setbacks, and more optimistic about the future.

Ultimately, the goal is not just to feel good in the moment but to rewire your emotional responses permanently. By consistently practicing gratitude, joy, hope, and mindfulness, you lay the foundation for a more resilient emotional state that can weather any storm.

Remember that building emotional resilience is not an overnight process. It's about cultivating small habits over time that gradually shift your emotional baseline toward positivity. But with consistent effort, you will experience profound changes in your emotional landscape, and you'll be able to navigate life's challenges with greater strength and ease.

The Power of Visualization: Reprogramming Your Emotional Future

The power of visualization is more than just a motivational tool—it's a neuroscientific strategy that can reshape your emotional responses and enhance your ability to control your emotions in the future. The process of visualizing positive outcomes isn't just about wishful thinking; it's about programming your brain to anticipate success, overcome challenges, and experience emotional growth. In this chapter, we will explore how visualization works on a neurobiological level, how it can be used to reprogram your emotional future, and practical techniques you can use to master your emotional state through focused mental imagery.

How the Brain Uses Visualization to Solidify Emotional Control

Visualization is a powerful tool because it taps into the brain's **neuroplasticity**—the ability of the brain to reorganize itself and form new neural connections in response to experience. When you visualize a specific emotional experience or outcome, you activate the same brain regions as if you were actually experiencing that event in real life. This happens because the brain doesn't distinguish between real and vividly imagined experiences when it comes to emotional responses. For example, when you imagine a situation that causes you anxiety—like speaking in public—your brain lights up the same neural networks that would be activated if you were truly standing in front of an audience.

On the flip side, when you visualize a positive emotional outcome, the brain also activates those networks, reinforcing the emotional responses that will be beneficial in real life. Over time, these repeated visualizations strengthen the neural pathways associated with calmness, confidence, and emotional control. This process essentially trains your brain to respond in a specific way when facing real-world situations, allowing you to gain more control over your emotions, rather than being at their mercy.

The brain's **mirror neurons** are also part of this process. Mirror neurons are specialized cells in the brain that help us mimic behaviors and emotions we see in others. They play a role in empathy, as they allow us to "mirror" the emotions and actions of others. When you visualize a desired emotional state, your brain activates the same neural networks it would if you were directly experiencing that emotional state. This process helps to solidify the emotional connections needed for effective emotional regulation.

Thus, visualization works by strengthening your brain's emotional responses and neural connections in a way that enhances emotional resilience and control.

Training Your Brain to Anticipate Positive Emotional Outcomes

Visualization doesn't just help you prepare for challenges—it helps you to anticipate positive outcomes. By focusing your mind on successful, calm, or empowering emotional responses, you begin to rewire your brain to default to those outcomes rather than fear, stress, or anxiety.

The **anticipation effect** is a crucial aspect of this. When you visualize success or emotional control, you're not just imagining what could happen; you're mentally rehearsing for success. For instance, if you've ever prepared for an important meeting, performance, or interview, you might have found that visualizing a confident, successful version of yourself leads to better outcomes. You've essentially prepared your brain for that success. Visualization builds mental habits and prepares you to experience emotions in the way you want to experience them.

The key here is that your brain doesn't recognize the difference between real and vividly imagined events. By regularly visualizing a successful outcome, you lay down the foundation for your brain to access those emotional states automatically when faced with similar situations in reality.

There's also a strong link between **dopamine** release and the process of anticipating success. Dopamine is the neurotransmitter that plays a critical role in reward-motivated behavior. When you visualize a positive outcome, your brain releases dopamine, essentially telling you that the anticipated outcome is rewarding. This release of dopamine encourages the behavior or emotional response you're visualizing, increasing the likelihood that you'll feel the same emotions when you encounter similar situations in real life. Over time, this can help you build emotional strength and the ability to manage emotions effectively.

Visualization Exercises for Mastering Specific Emotional States

To harness the power of visualization, it's important to practice with specific emotional outcomes in mind. Instead of general wishful thinking, you should create detailed mental images that are directly tied to your emotional goals. Whether you want to reduce anxiety, enhance confidence, or maintain emotional composure under stress, there are practical visualization exercises that can train your brain to perform in a way that serves those needs.

1. Overcoming Anxiety with Visualization

One of the most common emotional challenges people face is anxiety. Whether it's the anxiety of a public speaking event, an important exam, or a social situation, anxiety can hijack your ability to think clearly and act with confidence. The good news is that you can use visualization to change how your brain responds to these situations.

Exercise:

- Start by finding a quiet place to sit where you won't be disturbed. Close your eyes and take a few deep breaths to relax your body.
- Visualize the situation that usually triggers your anxiety. Imagine it as vividly as possible—picture the room, the people, the sounds, the environment.
- Now, instead of allowing the anxiety to take over, imagine yourself handling the situation with calm and control. Picture yourself speaking clearly, maintaining good posture, and feeling confident. Visualize your thoughts being clear and your body relaxed. See yourself succeeding and feeling proud of how you handled the situation.
- As you visualize this positive outcome, notice how your body feels. You may feel calmer, more relaxed, or empowered. Focus on that feeling and anchor it in your mind.
- Repeat this visualization daily, gradually increasing the vividness of the scenario and reinforcing the calm, confident version of yourself. Over time, your brain will be conditioned to respond with this same level of

calmness and confidence in real-life situations.

This exercise works because it retrains your brain to associate the situation with calm and confidence rather than anxiety. Over time, you'll find that your anxiety response weakens, and you'll be able to remain composed even in challenging situations.

2. Cultivating Confidence for High-Stakes Situations

Many people struggle with confidence when faced with high-stakes situations, such as job interviews, presentations, or any situation where performance is being evaluated. By visualizing success, you can strengthen your sense of self-assurance and prepare your brain to respond with confidence.

Exercise:

- Begin by closing your eyes and taking several deep breaths. Relax your body and clear your mind.
- Visualize the specific situation where you need confidence. Imagine yourself in that situation—whether it's walking into an interview, giving a speech, or making an important decision.
- Visualize yourself in a state of full confidence. Picture your posture as open and strong, your voice as clear and steady, and your thoughts as calm and focused. Imagine yourself succeeding and feeling proud of your performance.
- As you visualize, focus on the emotions you would experience during the successful outcome. Feel the **self-assurance** and **empowerment** that comes from knowing you handled the situation with ease.
- When you finish, take note of how your body feels. You may notice a sense of inner strength or confidence that wasn't there before.
- Revisit this exercise regularly, especially when you anticipate facing a similar situation. With repetition, your brain will associate these high-stakes scenarios with calm and confident emotional responses.

Visualization not only improves your emotional response in real-time but also helps build the emotional muscle necessary for long-term success. You're training your brain to access positive emotions, and the more you practice, the more automatic these responses will become.

3. Managing Anger or Frustration

Anger is an emotion that often leads to impulsive actions and regrettable decisions. However, visualization can be used to help you neutralize anger and replace it with more constructive emotional states, such as calm or understanding.

Exercise:

- Find a quiet space and close your eyes. Take a few deep breaths to center yourself.
- Picture a situation that normally triggers your anger or frustration. Visualize the people involved, the environment, and the events that unfold.
- Rather than allowing the anger to escalate, visualize yourself responding with calm and composure. See yourself taking a deep breath and choosing to pause before reacting. Picture your body relaxing, your mind clearing, and your emotions becoming more balanced.
- Imagine how you would speak in a calm, collected manner and how you would resolve the situation without letting your anger control you.
- As you rehearse this in your mind, focus on the positive emotions that arise from maintaining control—feel the satisfaction of handling the situation with maturity and poise.
- Repeat this visualization regularly, especially when you anticipate situations that could trigger anger. Over time, your brain will associate these situations with calm responses, and you will be less likely to be hijacked by anger in real life.

By practicing these visualizations regularly, you're essentially "training" your brain to remain calm in the face of stress and anger. With enough repetition, your emotional responses will change, making it easier for you to manage your emotions in challenging situations.

4. Visualizing Long-Term Emotional Mastery

Finally, visualization can be used not just for specific emotional situations but also for **long-term emotional growth**. By visualizing your ideal emotional state—whether it's peace, resilience, joy, or inner strength—you can reprogram your brain to cultivate these emotions over time.

Exercise:

- Sit quietly, close your eyes, and take several deep breaths.
- Visualize a version of yourself who is emotionally resilient, balanced, and composed no matter the situation. Picture yourself navigating life's challenges with grace, confidence, and emotional control.
- As you imagine this ideal version of yourself, focus on the feelings of peace, empowerment, and emotional freedom that arise. Notice how your mind and body feel in this state of emotional mastery.
- Take note of any specific qualities or characteristics that make this future version of you feel strong and emotionally balanced.
- Return to this visualization daily, reinforcing the idea that you can evolve into this more emotionally resilient version of yourself.

By making this long-term visualization a daily practice, you program your brain to move toward emotional mastery. Over time, you will begin to embody these qualities in your daily life, creating a lasting shift in how you manage your emotions.

Visualization is a powerful tool for emotional control because it allows you to **train** your brain to respond in positive ways to the situations you face. By rehearsing emotional mastery through vivid mental imagery, you can rewire your brain, build new neural pathways, and anticipate positive emotional outcomes. With regular practice, visualization helps you respond to challenges with confidence, calm, and composure, while also improving your long-term emotional resilience. The more you practice, the more automatic your emotional control becomes, allowing you to navigate life with greater ease and emotional strength.

Creating an Emotionally Autonomous Life: Living on Your Own Terms

In order to live an emotionally autonomous life, it's essential to understand that emotional freedom isn't just about reacting less to external stimuli; it's about creating a deep internal structure where your emotions no longer control you. Emotional autonomy means being able to think and act from your own authentic emotional center, not from the pressures, expectations, or moods of others. When you achieve this, your emotional responses become your choice, not a result of external influences or unconscious triggers. It's a state of complete emotional self-mastery.

We'll explore the key principles behind cultivating emotional independence, understand the role of neural feedback loops in maintaining that autonomy, and provide a roadmap to develop lifelong emotional mastery. The goal here is to help you build a strong, resilient emotional foundation so that external circumstances no longer dictate how you feel or react.

How to Cultivate Lasting Emotional Independence and Freedom

Emotional independence begins with self-awareness. When you are deeply attuned to your own emotional state, you can observe your reactions to situations without immediately being swept away by them. This awareness acts as the first step in creating emotional freedom because it gives you the power to choose how you respond.

At its core, emotional independence is about making the decision not to be a slave to your emotions. This doesn't mean suppressing your emotions or pretending they don't exist. On the contrary, emotional autonomy comes from **accepting and understanding** your emotions fully, and then choosing to act in alignment with your values, goals, and well-being—rather than simply reacting to whatever happens around you.

To break free from emotional dependency, the first step is to **detach your identity from your emotions**. Often, we see our emotions as who we are. We say things like, "I'm angry," or "I'm anxious." However, emotions are simply signals—they arise and fade. They don't define us. Realizing this is powerful because it gives you space between you and your emotions. You can acknowledge them without identifying with them.

The second key to emotional independence is **building emotional resilience**. Resilience is the ability to return to a balanced state after being emotionally disturbed. It's not about avoiding negative emotions; it's about having the ability to **recover quickly** when they arise, and to continue living according to your values, no matter what you feel in the moment. Building emotional resilience involves training your brain to handle emotional stress and bounce back from adversity, without letting it dictate your behavior.

1. Detaching from External Validation

The next part of achieving emotional independence is understanding your emotional reactions to external validation or approval. Many people derive their self-worth from how others perceive them. This creates a **cycle of dependence** where your emotions are constantly influenced by others' opinions and behaviors. This is a recipe for emotional instability because people's opinions are unpredictable.

Emotional autonomy means breaking free from this cycle. It's important to build your self-worth on your own terms, not based on the approval of others. The more you depend on external validation, the more you're subject to **emotional fluctuations** when that validation is withheld or rejected. This dependency makes you emotionally reactive and vulnerable.

To stop depending on others for emotional validation, develop **internal self-acceptance**. This means understanding that you are enough as you are. You don't need others to approve of you in order to feel complete. This inner confidence allows you to be immune to the emotional influence of external opinions and expectations.

2. Building Emotional Boundaries

Another critical component of emotional autonomy is establishing clear emotional boundaries. Emotional boundaries refer to the limits you set to protect yourself from being overwhelmed by others' emotions, behaviors, or needs. Without strong boundaries, you may find yourself constantly giving in to others, sacrificing your own emotional well-being in the process.

Creating emotional boundaries requires that you **acknowledge your emotional limits** and practice asserting them. If someone is constantly draining your emotional energy or making you feel bad about yourself, it's important to set a boundary. This doesn't mean cutting people off or becoming cold; rather, it's about making sure you don't absorb their emotional state as your own.

For example, if someone is angry and directs their anger toward you, an emotionally autonomous person would recognize that the anger is theirs, not theirs to carry. By mentally distancing yourself from others' emotions, you take away their power to affect your emotional state. This may involve saying "no" when necessary, avoiding toxic people or situations, or learning how to disengage from emotionally draining conversations.

The Role of Neural Feedback Loops in Maintaining Emotional Autonomy

One of the keys to emotional autonomy lies in how your brain **processes and reinforces emotional responses**. Your emotional brain is not just passive; it is constantly adapting to the world around you and creating neural pathways based on the experiences you have. Over time, your emotional brain forms **neural feedback loops**—self-reinforcing cycles that can either build or undermine your emotional autonomy.

For example, if you react to a stressful situation with fear, and that reaction leads to further stress or avoidance, your brain begins to associate fear with stress. This feedback loop strengthens, and the next time a similar situation arises, you are more likely to experience fear. The more this loop is reinforced, the harder it becomes to break out of it.

The good news is that neural feedback loops can also work in your favor. By intentionally reinforcing positive emotional responses, you can create **healthy feedback loops** that strengthen your ability to maintain emotional independence.

The key here is **conscious emotional regulation**. Each time you choose a calm, confident, or balanced emotional response, you reinforce the neural pathways associated with those emotional states. Over time, your brain will **shift** its default emotional responses, allowing you to act from a place of emotional autonomy, rather than reactivity.

This process is much like creating new neural habits. Just as it's difficult to change a habitual behavior (like biting your nails), it's difficult to change deeply ingrained emotional reactions. However, with consistent practice and intentional effort, you can **reprogram your emotional brain**.

1. Rewiring Emotional Responses Through Repetition

To change your emotional responses, it's important to repeat the new behavior or emotional state regularly. This process is similar to training for a sport or learning a musical instrument—**consistent practice leads to mastery**. In the case of emotional autonomy, this practice involves making a deliberate choice to respond calmly or confidently in emotional situations, and reinforcing that choice over time.

The more you practice emotional regulation, the more likely it is that you will **automatically choose the healthier, more balanced emotional response** when faced with stress or adversity. This reduces the chances of being hijacked by intense emotions like anger, fear, or anxiety. Eventually, your brain will begin to rely on these new neural pathways, creating a solid foundation for emotional autonomy.

2. Creating Emotional Feedback Loops for Resilience

The key to resilience is creating emotional feedback loops that reinforce your **ability to recover from adversity**. Rather than being thrown off course by negative events, you learn to bounce back quickly and return to a calm state. These positive feedback loops are formed by consistently practicing emotional resilience.

Let's take an example: when you face a stressful situation, instead of allowing anxiety or frustration to take over, you consciously choose to remain calm. Over time, your brain will start to **associate stressful situations with calmness** rather than anxiety. This mental shift will make it easier to stay grounded, even in the face of future stressors.

The more you practice emotional resilience, the more you will notice yourself **bouncing back from challenges** with greater ease. This shift in your brain's default emotional response is what will allow you to live on your own terms, without being ruled by external events or the emotions of others.

Developing a Lifelong Practice for Emotional Mastery

Achieving emotional autonomy is not a one-time event; it's a lifelong practice. While you can make significant progress in a short period of time, maintaining emotional independence requires consistent effort and mindfulness. Here's how to build a sustainable practice for emotional mastery:

1. Regular Self-Reflection

Self-reflection is a cornerstone of emotional mastery. It allows you to become aware of your emotional patterns and identify areas where you may still be reactive. By regularly checking in with yourself, you can catch negative emotional patterns early and adjust before they gain momentum.

Make it a habit to **reflect daily on your emotional responses**. At the end of each day, take a few minutes to ask yourself: "What emotions did I experience today? How did I respond to them? Was my reaction aligned with my goals or values?" This practice will help you gain insight into your emotional landscape and identify areas where you may need to apply more focus or change.

2. Consistent Mindfulness Practice

Mindfulness is one of the most effective tools for emotional mastery. It helps you to be aware of your emotions without being consumed by them. Through mindfulness, you can observe your emotions as they arise and make the conscious decision not to act on them impulsively. Over time, mindfulness helps you develop a **greater sense of emotional awareness** and control.

Make mindfulness a part of your daily routine. Whether through meditation, deep breathing, or simply paying attention to your emotions throughout the day, mindfulness will help you stay centered and emotionally autonomous.

3. Commit to Lifelong Emotional Growth

Emotional autonomy is not about perfection; it's about continuous improvement. Your emotional growth should be seen as a lifelong journey, not a destination. Continue to challenge yourself by embracing new emotional challenges, refining your emotional responses, and growing in emotional strength.

Be patient with yourself, but also stay committed to the process. With time and consistent effort, you will find that emotional autonomy becomes not just a practice, but a way of life.

Conclusion

As you've now seen, mastering your emotions isn't a matter of simply trying to suppress or avoid them. **Emotions are integral parts of who we are as human beings**—they provide us with the ability to connect with others, experience joy, and make decisions based on our deeper instincts. However, when our emotions control us instead of the other way around, they can cloud our judgment, distort our perception of reality, and lead to outcomes that we later regret. It's the difference between being a passive observer in your own life, carried along by a current of feelings you can't control, and being the one in charge of the helm, steering yourself wherever you choose to go.

The understanding of the **neurobiology of emotions** and the tools outlined in this book have shown you that emotional freedom is not an abstract or impossible dream. It is a **practical skill**—one that you can cultivate by applying certain principles, mental practices, and strategies. But as with any skill, emotional mastery requires consistent, deliberate practice. In this conclusion, we will revisit the core insights of the book, solidify the key practices you need to implement, and emphasize the lifelong commitment to emotional autonomy that can truly transform your life.

Emotions Are Powerful Forces, But They Don't Have to Rule You

The first step in this journey is accepting that emotions are inevitable, but they don't have to be your master. **Your emotions are not inherently good or bad.** They are simply signals, biological responses to stimuli that have evolved to keep us alive and guide us through the world. Yet, in our modern society, we often find ourselves trapped by those same emotional reactions. The rush of anxiety before a public speaking event, the anger in a heated argument, the depression following a difficult failure—these emotions often push us to react impulsively, without thinking, and shape the decisions we make, sometimes with harmful consequences.

What's critical to understand is that **the brain's emotional responses are not set in stone**. As you've seen through the discussions of neuroplasticity and emotional regulation, the brain can be rewired. The neural pathways that trigger emotional responses, whether they are grounded in fear, anger, sadness, or joy, are not permanent. **You have the power to change your emotional habits**, and that begins with awareness. By understanding how your brain processes emotions, how it responds to triggers, and how it forms patterns, you can interrupt the cycle before it takes hold.

The mistake most people make is believing that emotions control them, and therefore, they must either suppress their emotions or simply react to them. **This is the path to emotional enslavement**, where external circumstances dictate your internal experience. But you can choose to break this cycle. **You can choose to reclaim your emotional power**.

The Role of Awareness and Conscious Decision-Making

Throughout this book, one of the recurring themes has been the importance of awareness. Awareness is the first step to emotional freedom because it allows you to recognize when your emotions are taking control. Whether it's a fleeting moment of irritation, the gnawing sensation of anxiety, or the deep pull of sadness, the key to emotional autonomy lies in being able to observe those feelings without being consumed by them.

It's easy to react impulsively. When we feel stressed, we snap at others. When we feel anxious, we avoid the situation that causes discomfort. But through **mindfulness, cognitive reframing, and emotional detachment**, you can create the mental space needed to respond with intention, not reaction. **This space is where your true power lies**. It's the moment between stimulus and response where you get to decide: "How do I want to handle this?"

Building awareness requires practice. You won't always catch yourself in the heat of the moment. But the more you practice self-reflection, mindfulness, and emotional regulation techniques, the quicker you'll catch yourself the next time you feel a trigger rising. **Every time you pause and make a conscious decision to choose your response, you strengthen your ability to control your emotions.** Over time, this becomes second nature.

It's not enough to simply understand the mechanics of your brain and emotions. **What matters is putting that knowledge into practice.** This means integrating what you've learned here into your daily life, making these concepts part of who you are and how you approach the world.

Emotional Mastery Is a Continuous Journey

You may have noticed throughout this book that emotional mastery is framed not as a destination, but as a lifelong journey. This is a crucial point to understand. While you can make significant progress and experience dramatic shifts in your emotional life, **you will never reach a place where emotional challenges no longer arise**. Life is unpredictable, and stressors, triggers, and challenging situations will always be a part of your existence.

What makes emotional autonomy powerful, though, is that you no longer have to be at the mercy of these events. As you continue to practice the techniques of self-regulation, mindfulness, and emotional awareness, you will find that **you recover faster from emotional upheaval**, and you will be less likely to be drawn into destructive emotional spirals. **The goal isn't to eliminate negative emotions—it's to ensure that those emotions don't control your behavior or disrupt your peace of mind.**

The more you apply these practices—whether it's using the "pause" technique to create a moment of choice, recognizing and neutralizing anger, or practicing gratitude and positivity—the stronger the emotional muscles you build. This will form the foundation of your emotional resilience, which will carry you through difficult moments with greater ease and confidence.

The fact is, **you are the architect of your emotional life.** You design your reactions, your patterns, and your resilience. No one else controls how you feel unless you allow them to. Life may throw challenges your way, but your emotional state is something you have the power to shape, again and again.

Building a Life of Emotional Autonomy: Practical, Tangible Steps

To live an emotionally autonomous life, you need practical, everyday strategies. Over the course of this book, I've outlined a variety of techniques that are designed not to be theoretical, but **immediately applicable**. Here, I'll summarize some of the most important takeaways that you can begin to implement right away:

1. **Mindfulness**: Start with mindfulness practices to increase your awareness of your emotions as they arise. This can be as simple as taking a few moments each day to sit quietly and observe your

emotional state, without judgment. Over time, mindfulness will allow you to create that critical space between stimulus and response, giving you the ability to choose your actions.

2. **The Pause Technique**: This is one of the most effective tools you can use to interrupt emotional reactions. When you feel yourself becoming emotionally charged, take a second to pause. **In that brief moment of stillness, you have the power to decide whether to react impulsively or respond mindfully.** This simple pause creates the space you need to make the best decision.
3. **Emotional Detachment**: Understand that your emotions are not who you are. They are simply signals. Practice detaching your sense of identity from your emotional state. Recognize when you're allowing someone else's emotions to influence yours, and take back control. Remember: you do not need to internalize other people's emotional states.
4. **Cognitive Reframing**: Learn to reframe negative thoughts and emotions. If you're feeling anxious, challenge those thoughts and reframe them. **What evidence do you have that this fear is real? What's the worst that could happen, and how likely is it?** Reframing negative thoughts into neutral or positive ones can help neutralize the power of destructive emotions.
5. **Self-Compassion**: One of the most important practices for emotional autonomy is learning to be compassionate with yourself. **You will not be perfect.** There will be moments when you lose control or feel overwhelmed. The goal is not to avoid these moments, but to accept them without self-criticism, and then use them as learning experiences.
6. **Creating Boundaries**: Establish clear emotional boundaries in your relationships and your environment. If someone or something consistently drains your emotional energy or disturbs your peace, it's time to set a boundary. This can be difficult, but it is essential for maintaining your emotional autonomy.
7. **Positive Visualization**: Use the power of visualization to train your brain to respond in positive ways to emotional challenges. Visualizing calm, confident responses to stressors allows your brain to rehearse

these responses, so when you face real challenges, your emotional resilience is ready.

Your Future: Emotional Freedom Awaits

The truth is that emotional autonomy is more than just a mental skill—it is a way of living. It is about being free from the emotional burdens that weigh you down, from the unconscious triggers that pull your strings, and from the reactive patterns that hold you back from becoming the best version of yourself. **Emotional freedom means taking full responsibility for your emotional state.** It means becoming the person who is no longer a victim of their feelings, but someone who can calmly and clearly navigate the turbulence of life with confidence, resilience, and peace of mind.

The tools are here. The knowledge is here. The power is within you. The question now is, **what will you do with it?**

Take the first step. Make the choice to begin today. You are not bound by your emotions. You are the one in control.

www.ingramcontent.com/pod-product-compliance
Lightning Source LLC
LaVergne TN
LVHW022107200926
848481LV00003B/1094